Surviving the Heartbreak

of Choosing Death

For Your Pet

Linda M. Peterson

GREENTREE PUBLISHING

For information contact

Linda M. Peterson
239 Greentree Drive
West Chester, PA. 19382

TEL: (610) 399-3168
FAX: (610) 399-3168

Published in the United States of America

Library of Congress Catalog Card Number: 96-94369
ISBN 0-9652572-2-3
$12.95 Softcover; Includes bibliography and index

Cover design and illustration by Lightbourne Images, copyright © 1997

Printed by Thomson-Shore in the United States of America

This book may be ordered directly from Linda M. Peterson for $12.95 (U.S.), plus $3.00 shipping and handling (PA residents must add 6% sales tax on total. Please submit $16.90). Check or money order accepted.

This book is lovingly dedicated to...

The cherished memory of Ginny,
who helped me learn that euthanasia can be the kindest death

and

to all the courageous humans
who have struggled with the most difficult decision
any animal lover ever has to make

and

to all our departed animal friends
whose memories live on in our hearts.

CONTENTS

iv

Part II: DECISION-MAKING INFORMATION

Part III: SELF-CARE DURING PET EUTHANASIA

Part IV: AFTER THE EUTHANASIA

The Rainbow Bridge

Just this side of Heaven is a bridge of many colors called the Rainbow Bridge. At death, any animal who has a close connection with a human goes to Rainbow Bridge. There our pets find warm springtime weather, lots of food and water, and lush green meadows where they can run and play together. The old and frail are restored to health and vigor; those who are hurt or maimed are made whole again, just as we remember them in days gone by.

They are all happy and content, except for one small thing – they each miss their own special person who was left behind on Earth.

The day finally comes when one suddenly stops playing and looks into the distance. The bright eyes are intent; the nose twitches; the eager body begins to quiver. Suddenly your pet breaks from the group, flying over the green grass faster and faster.

You have been spotted, and when you and your special friend meet, you cling together in joyous reunion, never to be parted again. The happy kisses rain upon your face; your hands caress the beloved head, and you look once more into those trusting eyes, so long gone from your life, but never absent from your heart.

Then you cross the Rainbow Bridge together, never again to be separated.

- Author Unknown

Acknowledgments

To the very special professionals who helped in various ways with this book: Dr. Harvey Yenkinson, VMD, who compassionately helped Ginny leave this life; Dr. Darrell Hoffman, VMD, who helped with Ginny's final illness, and provided clinical information on small animal euthanasia procedures; Dr. Mark Donaldson, VMD, who supplied information on horse euthanasia; and Kim Rubio, veterinarian technician, who gave me detailed information on euthanasia procedures.

To all the pet owners whose pet euthanasia experiences convinced me of the need for this book. Most of their names and experiences have been altered to preserve confidentiality. Special thanks to the following whose names and experiences have not been disguised: Marie Ballantyne, Melton Berube, John and Daisy Czyscon, Suzanne Durboraw, Nellie Forman, George Gardner, Margaret Gregory, Betty Keegan, Donna McCabe, Sharla Roussel, Marge Wood, and Wanda and Tony Yula.

To Susan Lerke, Darlene McCoy, Betty McKinney and Terri Latril who reviewed the manuscript and offered invaluable feedback and suggestions. To Marion Williams, Nancy Aldrich, and Bobbi Baker whose support kept me going. To Dawn Robinson, our Saturday artist-in-resident, for cover suggestions. To Christine Blanke, of Thomson-Shore printers, who introduced me to the unknown world of printing. To Shannon Bodie, Lightbourne Images, who translated my sketchy ideas into the perfect book cover.

To the most important person, my husband, David, who expanded the rainbow on the cover, could figure out how to get around computer goofs, put in the doors and arrows, and helped tremendously with the final formatting and editing of the manuscript. Thanks for always being on call, but giving me space to write.

To my animal buddies, who were always at my feet while I was writing, and to their ancestor, Ginny, who inspired this book.

ABOUT THE AUTHOR

For the past 17 years, Linda Peterson has counseled bereaved pet owners, individually and in groups. Linda draws on her love of animals, her personal experience with pet loss, and her professional training in bereavement as she counsels her clients. In her psychotherapy practice, Linda also helps adults and children deal with a wide variety of other traumatic life, loss, and relationship problems.

A Board Certified Diplomate in clinical social work, Linda is licensed in Pennsylvania and Delaware. She is a member of the Academy of Certified Social Workers, the National Association of Social Workers, the Association for Death Education and Counseling, and the Employee Assistance Professionals Association. She is an officer of the William Penn Poodle Club.

Linda's close connection with animals began in rural upstate New York where she grew up, and has continued as she and her husband have raised and shown their *Amberspark* line of toy poodles.

Linda and her husband, David, live near Philadelphia with their dogs, two cats, and a bird..

Warning and Disclaimer

The information in this book is designed to supplement, not substitute for, the advice and directions of your vet, physician or psychotherapist. You should not make changes in any current treatment without first consulting your own trained medical professional. The author and publisher disclaim all liability and responsibility to any person or entity with respect to any loss or damage caused, or alleged to be caused, directly or indirectly by information in this book.

If you do not wish to be bound by the above, you may return this book to the publisher for a full refund.

INTRODUCTION

The winter of 1994 went on forever. And my dog, Ginny, was dying. Her eyesight and most of her mind left during that winter, but her body lived on. I avoided the thought of euthanasia for Ginny. Like most pet owners, I was sure I would never have to make *that* decision for *my* pet. She would just die peacefully in her sleep. But she didn't. And the day finally came when I knew I would have to take responsibility and help Ginny die.

How do you make a euthanasia decision for someone you love? How do you resolve your guilt so it doesn't continue to haunt you? It felt so wrong to think about killing Ginny and, yet, how long could I watch needless suffering when I knew I had the power to end that suffering? Furthermore, I felt I had an obligation to arrange a peaceful death for Ginny.

Logic told me to make the decision, end Ginny's suffering, and put the experience behind me. But emotions took over and logic went out the window. Intense feelings were stirred up about so many difficult issues: death, killing, relationship loss, and the abuse of power. Feelings about these issues created emotional blocks that interfered with logical decision-making. Being a psychotherapist, I realized I would have to deal with these feelings in conjunction with the decision-making process. If I ignored my feelings, they would continue to haunt me long after the euthanasia.

As I faced the two parts of the euthanasia experience – making the decision and dealing with my feelings – I realized there were no guidelines about how to do either one. The euthanasia dilemma has no right or wrong answer. Given exactly the same situation, you might decide to choose death for your pet at a different time than I would, or you might decide not to euthanize at all. And who could say that one person was right, and the other was wrong? Euthanasia is a very personal decision. But, without set guidelines, guilt easily creeps in. Pet euthanasia can leave you feeling as though you have violated your pet's trust, or somehow abused your power.

How do you sort all this out, and arrive at a state of mind where you can justify either your part in your pet's death, or your decision to let your pet die naturally? This book, which grew out of my euthanasia experience with Ginny, will help you think through what decision-making guidelines to use so you can justify your decision to yourself.

In addition, it will help you resolve the troubling feelings that euthanasia stirs up for animal lovers. It will guide you through the pain of facing reality and letting go, of making difficult decisions, and dealing with your guilt, fear, grief and anger. It will reduce your anxiety as it: 1) breaks down the euthanasia experience into small steps, 2) identifies what thoughts and feelings to expect at each step, 3) suggests how to deal with those thoughts and feelings, 4) outlines, in the *TAKE ACTION* sections, actions you can take to overcome that helpless feeling, and regain a sense of control, and 5) helps you adjust to life after the death of your pet.

Throughout the book, I have alternated the masculine and feminine pronouns *he* and *she* in recognition that pets are both male and female. Although I use the term *pet owners*, I acknowledge that our animal companions really own their significant humans.

Society tries to discount the trauma of pet euthanasia. But every animal lover knows the feelings it stirs up cannot be lightly dismissed. Are you currently considering euthanasia for your pet? Did you choose euthanasia for a pet in the past? Are you struggling with unresolved feelings of grief, fear, anger or guilt? Whatever your situation, I hope this book will help you overcome any emotional blocks so that you can resolve your feelings about euthanasia.

Pet euthanasia is an experience we all want to avoid. But when faced with it, we want to be able to make a decision we feel comfortable with. May this book guide you in your search for wisdom and courage to make the right decision. May it validate your decision, comfort you in your loss, and help you survive the heartbreak of choosing death for *your* pet.

Linda Peterson
October 1996

PART I

THE EUTHANASIA EXPERIENCE

CHAPTER 1

Hiding Behind Your Myths

July 3rd that year was delightfully warm and sunny, the kind of day that makes you happy just to be alive. Even my cat, Willow, usually an unwilling traveler, purred contentedly as we drove along the winding country road toward Doc's office. Maybe she knew she only had an eye infection and wasn't scheduled for any shots.

Despite the early morning hour, Doc's waiting room was already filling up when I arrived. Across from me sat a dejected looking man and his young son. The boy, crying softly, reached down to get a reassuring lick from their dog, a personable Basset Hound with soulful brown eyes, named Barney.

Curiosity overcame me, and I asked what was wrong with Barney. The man confided that yesterday the cancer specialist had told them Barney's cancer was out of control and nothing more could be done. In just a few minutes Barney had an appointment to die. The man swallowed hard. The boy hung his head and looked miserable. Completely unaware of the tragic scene that revolved around him, Barney looked toward the door, wagged his tail, and sniffed at an incoming dog.

Suddenly I felt freezing cold. I hugged Willow too tightly and tried to think of something comforting to say besides, "I'm so sorry." But what do you say to a father and son with a dog facing death? Instead of talking, I quietly listened as they told me about this terrible tragedy that had befallen their dear friend, Barney.

We all jumped a little when *their* name was called. I watched them shakily walk Barney into the examining room and eternity. The father said to Doc, "We saw the cancer specialist. There is nothing more that can be done..." And then the door slammed shut on the scene.

Left in the waiting room, I tried to think about something besides what was happening on the other side of that door. But it was impossible. I found myself praying that all my pets would just die in their sleep. How do you go about making the decision Barney's people had just made for him? How do you choose death for someone you love?

In a few minutes, that seemed like hours, the father and son came out without Barney. The father reached over and sympathetically ruffled his young son's crewcut as they walked very fast to the car with their heads down.

After the heartbroken man and boy left, I talked to Doc about Willow's eye infection as though nothing unusual had happened. But, deep inside, the feeling of horror continued as I tried to avoid the thought that someday it might be my pet who was terminally ill.

On my way home from Doc's office, I tried to erase the intense feelings of the euthanasia scene I had stumbled into that day. After all, my pets were in good health, weren't they? So I told myself, "It won't happen to me." And I felt fairly reassured that, indeed, it would never happen to me.

Just in case, for a little extra reassurance, I nailed shut the door between life and death with a few spikes I call "myths." "My pet will die peacefully in his sleep" or "Modern medicine can keep my pet alive if she becomes ill" gave me a false sense of security as long as my pets were in good health.

A diagram of the use of myths would look like this:

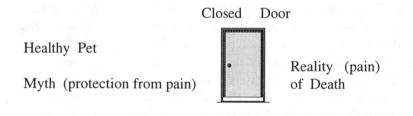

Death and euthanasia are on the other side of the closed door when your pet is healthy, and you use myths to make sure the door stays closed. Occasionally the door opens for a brief moment and you peek through it, as we did during the scene in Doc's office. But you quickly close it. And this is as it should be. Who wants to think about the sadness of death before being faced with it?

There will come a time, hopefully far in the future, when you will have to move beyond the myths and face the reality of death. To prepare yourself for that future time, let's look at some of the more popular myths and the realities behind them that we all avoid facing while our pet is healthy. You may feel uncomfortable, fearful, or even angry, as you read the next few pages. You are taking the first step toward starting to seriously consider euthanasia for your pet. It is a difficult, but important step.

Myth # 1:   My Pet Will Die Peacefully In His Sleep After a Long Loving Life.

If you allow yourself to think about your pet's death, you probably picture your pet dying an easy, painless death after a very long life, preferably at home in his sleep. You are sure you will never even have to consider euthanasia for your pet.

But it's difficult to dispel the uneasy feelings after that euthanasia scene at Doc's office. How many people or pets do you know who died peacefully in their sleep without prior suffering? Deep inside, you know that life scripts don't always work out the way you plan them. Illness, old age, accidental injury, or an inability to care for a beloved pet: there are many routes by which any of us suddenly could face the unthinkable — an euthanasia decision for *our* pet.

The reality is that few pets, who are elderly or terminally ill, die easily and painlessly in their sleep without prior suffering. A natural death is seldom a pain-free death.

Jane had always assumed her 19-year old cat, Emily, would just die peacefully in her sleep someday. At her age, Emily did sleep most of the time, but she always woke up. Then Emily stopped eating. Following a diagnosis of incurable cancer, Jane realized she had to move beyond her myth of Emily dying peacefully in her sleep. She had to face reality, and consider choosing death for Emily.

TAKE ACTION. Use this book to understand what it will be like for you if you need to consider euthanasia for your pet. What will happen? How will you feel? How can you best get through it?

Myth # 2:   Modern Medicine Can Keep My Pet Alive So I Won't Have to Consider Euthanasia.

Most of us view death as a medical failure. We expect modern medicine to cure our pet, or at least keep him alive and pain-free, so we won't have to consider euthanasia.

If medical treatment improves your pet's health temporarily, you will not move beyond this myth very quickly. You may even try to use this extra time to fool yourself into thinking that your pet is cured and will not die. Such thinking will leave you unprepared when your pet eventually starts to suffer and needs to be euthanized.

Connected with this myth are major decisions about medical intervention. You will need to decide *how much* medical care you want to arrange for your pet.

There are three realities about modern medicine care:

1. It has limits. It will not be able to cure an elderly or terminally ill pet. It may sometimes be able to prolong life, and to buy you a little more time with your pet.

2. There is no guarantee that medical treatment will extend life, or postpone your need to make the euthanasia decision. Some pets respond well to treatment. Some don't. Ask your veterinarian how well other animals have responded to the same treatment. You need to prepare yourself in the event that the medical treatment is not as successful as you had hoped.

3. Sometimes, extensive medical testing and treatment can make dying more lengthy and uncomfortable. Veterinary medicine has made advances in treating formerly untreatable medical conditions. But don't rush into choosing the most extensive medical tests or treatments. Take time to ask questions. Consider the expense. Ask whether the treatments will really extend your pet's life, or just increase his suffering as he moves toward death.

How long should I fight to prolong my pet's life? Once you get beyond the myth that medical intervention will save your pet's life, how long you fight to prolong life is a very personal decision. Some people may need to know that they have fought against death by using everything veterinary medicine has to offer their pet, so they will have no regrets later. Others feel comfortable choosing just enough medical care to prevent suffering. Is extensive medical care one of your priorities? There is no right or wrong answer. Only you can decide.

TAKE ACTION. *1) Take time to question your veterinarian carefully, as outlined in Chapter 13, so you know what to expect before making your decision about medical treatment. Will medical tests/treatment really help your pet or extend his life? Consult the decision-making model in Chapter 14 to help make a decision about the amount of medical care you want to give your dying pet.*

2) Use the extra time modern medicine gives your pet to say goodbye and let go. Prepare yourself for her death, and for your part in that death.

Myth # 3:   Natural Death In a Technological Age is Easier Than Death In the Wild or Death by Euthanasia.

You protect your pet from predators and contagious diseases that killed his wild ancestors. When he becomes ill, you get him high tech medical attention. You feed him if he's too weak to eat. In the wild, an animal, weakened by age or illness, is killed by predators or goes off by himself, doesn't eat, and dies.

As you protect your pet from the type of death he would have in the wild, and give him the best medical care, you set up a situation in which a natural death can be a long, drawn-out, and painful process. You also create a dilemma in which your pet's suffering may lead you to consider euthanasia – to give your pet the very death that you have fought to save your pet from up to that point.

Euthanasia, coming from two Greek words, *eu* meaning "well" and *thanatos* meaning "death," literally means an easy death or way of dying. Euthanasia is a gentler death for your pet than either death in the wild or a natural death. It is the way your pet can lose consciousness and die swiftly with dignity and without pain. Isn't that the kind of death we all want for our loved ones?

It is true that you will have to be involved. But, as you start to see the suffering that occurs while waiting for a natural death, it will become easier for you to accept your part in choosing euthanasia for one you love.

The reality is that "natural death" in a technological age is not an easy death. In fact, it is a prolonged death due to the medical procedures that can keep the body alive, and the lack of natural predators that would quickly kill a sick animal in the wild.

The reality is that, true to it's meaning, the procedure called euthanasia is the way you can give your pet a quick, pain-free death in the technological age.

Jim used every medical test and treatment available to prolong his dog's life after Bear was diagnosed with kidney disease. When the doctors could do no more, he hand-fed him, and carried him around in a cart because he couldn't walk. Bear would have died, or been killed, months ago in the wild. The longer Bear lived, the more he suffered. Finally, Jim realized he had to let go and help Bear do the very thing he had fought against for so long. He had to help Bear die.

Step 1 of the Euthanasia Experience.   Using myths to avoid thoughts of your pet's death is the first step in what I call the "euthanasia experience."

There are three different types of euthanasia experiences which we will consider in the next chapter. Although each type has its own distinct features, the use of myths is the first step in all three experiences.

TAKE ACTION.   Identify which myths you use to avoid facing the realities connected with death. Do you use different myths than the three discussed in this chapter?

CHAPTER 2

Three Types of Euthanasia Experiences

The euthanasia experience is a life experience during which:

♦ You accept the reality that your pet is going to die.
♦ You accept euthanasia as the kindest death for your pet.
♦ You accept your part in the euthanasia without excessive guilt.

Until you deal with your feelings about all three parts of this experience, you may not feel at peace with the euthanasia.

There are three types of euthanasia experiences:

♦ A long-term euthanasia experience, which usually involves a terminal illness or bodily deterioration from old age.

♦ Emergency euthanasia: usually the result of a serious accidental injury that is financially catastrophic or not repairable.

♦ Euthanasia of a healthy pet due to unresolvable behavior or temperament problems, or the pet owner's inability to continue to care for the pet. The euthanasia of a healthy pet can be either a long-term or an emergency experience.

Throughout this book we will consider how to deal with the unique characteristics and problems of each type of euthanasia experience.

The Steps of the Euthanasia Experience.

There are seven steps in the euthanasia experience. They are not like normal steps that quickly lead you to your destination. You will find yourself repeatedly moving back and forth between the steps as you slowly descend them and focus on the emotional work that awaits you at each step. You might find yourself working primarily on one step. But, at the same time, you might be working with less intensity on several steps. You might even retrace your steps, if you need to do a little more work on a particular step. For example, you might go back into a myth after moving beyond it, or hold on to you pet after letting go.

For example, when my veterinarian was preparing to give Ginny the injection to end her life, I retreated to my favorite myth as I asked how she would die if I let her die naturally. His answer confirmed that a natural death would be too painful for Ginny, and moved me beyond that myth for the final time.

The seven steps of the euthanasia experience are:

Hiding Behind Your Myths
Myth-Holding Onto Pet-Pain Circle
Facing Reality
Letting Go of Your Pet and Relationship
Choosing Death For Your Pet
Mourning the Lost Relationship
Adjusting to Life Without Your Pet

How The Timing of Euthanasia Impacts The Grief Process.
A long-term euthanasia experience will give you the most time to move through the first four steps prior to your pet's death. Therefore, with a terminally ill or elderly pet, you will usually be quite far along in the grief process by the time you choose death for your animal friend.

If you are facing an emergency euthanasia, you will not have sufficient time to appropriately deal with your feelings about any of the steps prior to death. Therefore, after an emergency euthanasia, most of the grief work is still waiting for you following the death. However, releasing your grief may be complicated because it is more difficult to grieve without the physical presence of the deceased. Also, our society is not very supportive of mourning after the death of a pet. People will probably give you the message, "Out of sight, out of mind." Even so, rise to the challenge and express your grief. Until you do, it will always be inside you ready to pop out at awkward moments.

The complicating part of a long-term euthanasia experience that lasts months or years is that you are put under the stress of looking through the open door into reality a long time before you are at the step where you need to end your pet's life. Refer to Chapter 17 for suggestions on dealing with this kind of stress.

A second complication of a long-term euthanasia experience is that, as you watch your pet survive one health crisis after another, you may not do the necessary emotional letting-go work because you expect him to continue surviving his medical crises. Try to use the time of a long-term euthanasia experience to work on letting go.

Dianna's cat, Beethoven, was slowing dying from kidney disease. Whenever he had a relapse, Dianna was put under the stress of considering euthanasia. This continued for several years until Beethoven went into his final medical crisis, and Dianna decided to help him die. Beethoven's lengthy illness gave Dianna time to work on all her feelings about her cat's death and euthanasia, and she did just that. But the years of continuing stress left her exhausted.

Duration Of The Euthanasia Experience. The euthanasia experience continues until you come to some kind of peace with your part in the euthanasia, and adjust to a changed life without your pet's physical presence. Yes, this experience can continue long after the death of your pet, if you have lingering guilt, anger, or depression after the euthanasia. Most people, who are still grieving deeply months after their pet's death, have additional work to do on one or more of the steps listed above. This is especially common following an emergency euthanasia, when you have to deal with most of your feelings following the death.

In the following chapters, we will look more closely at each of the steps you will go through during a euthanasia experience.

TO THINK ABOUT . _During a lengthy illness, you will have time to resolve many of your feelings before the euthanasia, but you will have long-term stress._

After an emergency euthanasia, you will have to resolve most of your feelings following the death. But it will be difficult to grieve sufficiently once the death has taken place.

CHAPTER 3

The Myth-Holding Onto Pet-Pain Circle

In the long-term euthanasia experience, you move from *hiding behind your myths* (Step 1) to *the myth-holding on to pet-pain circle* (Step 2) when you learn your pet is dying.

It may seem like an insignificant problem at first. You find a small bump on your dog's leg, or your cat looks thin and won't eat, or your horse goes lame. The problem doesn't go away, and you decide to check with your veterinarian. With a worried expression on his face, your veterinarian tells you that he has some bad news for you . . . your pet is seriously ill, and suffering will precede your pet's death. One of your options, at some time in the future, is euthanasia – choosing death for your pet.

In that instant your life changes. The door between life and death and myth and reality swings open. As you stand in that doorway, you realize, perhaps for the first time, that your pet is going to die, and you may even have to help her die.

Since there is no emergency, your first instinct is to hold on just a little longer to the myths that have protected you from painful reality for so long. And you probably will do just that. You will hear yourself saying, "It can't be true. There has to be some treatment that will cure this problem. My pet doesn't seem that sick. I'm sure she will die in her sleep."

At this point, the door to reality has opened. You know what the reality is, but you are not yet ready to go through that open door and face reality. You choose to remain on the myth side of the open door for now. You are in what I call the *myth-holding on to pet-pain circle*.
A diagram of what you are going through would look like this:

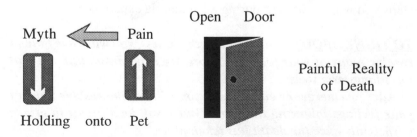

In Step 2, when you comprehend the reality that your pet is dying, the myths are no longer effective in shielding you from painful feelings. On the contrary, the myths will bring you pain if you hold on to them now.

As long as you believe the myths, you will have expectations that events will turn out the way the myths say they will. You will fight unsuccessfully to keep your dying pet alive, or wait for an easy natural death that doesn't happen.

As your dying pet's condition worsens, you will feel frustrated and helpless. You will find it very painful to watch someone you love suffer, and not be able to help. It is frustrating when you are putting forth your best efforts, all to no avail.

How will I feel in the myth-holding onto pet-pain circle?
You will feel numbness, a sense of unreality, despair, fear, loss-of-control, grief and anger. You will try to deny or avoid the feelings.

What actions can I take while I'm in the myth-holding onto pet-pain circle? Taking action is a good idea because it will help you feel more in control. Gather information and make decisions about medical care (See Section II). Do everything you can to work toward the outcome you want for your pet, so you will have no regrets later. Give your pet excellent medical care or home nursing, Talk to friends about their similar experiences and about what you are going through and feeling. Write about your feelings. Remember you are not alone in your feelings.

It is possible to stay in this myth-holding onto pet-pain stage for quite a period of time, if your pet has an illness that progresses slowly. With a protracted illness or an aged pet, you will move back and forth through the doorway between myth and reality numerous times as you gradually face reality.

Why does it take so long to face reality? When you read the various myths and the realities behind them, intellectually you quickly recognize the truths behind each of the myths. *But intellectually acknowledging the reality and emotionally accepting the reality are two different things.* Your logical mind works at a more rapid rate than your feelings. Your feelings take time. Because your feelings don't want to accept the reality, you will test reality by trying to disprove it. This testing process will delay your moving through the door into reality.

The way you will test the reality is by trying to take actions to resolve the problem. It will take you time to realize your efforts aren't working. Eventually, your unsuccessful efforts will convince you that the reality stands. At that point, you will move from myth to reality. The speed at which you move into reality will vary with each individual.

What can I do to accept the reality that my pet is going to die?
It's difficult to plan how your pet will die until you have accepted the reality that he *is going* to die. You will move toward accepting your pet's death as you:

1) Think about it
2) Talk about it
3) Write about it
4) See physical evidence of illness
5) See evidence that your attempts to cure your pet's health problems are unsuccessful

When Lisa's horse, Blackjack, was diagnosed with progressive heart disease, both her veterinarian and her friends suggested that Lisa consider the possibility of helping Blackjack die. Intellectually Lisa heard what the veterinarian and her friends said, but emotionally she had not yet accepted her horse's death. Since Lisa was still in the myth-holding onto pet-pain circle, she was not really far enough along in the process to make a sound euthanasia decision. How could she plan Blackjack's death when she had not yet accepted the fact that Blackjack was going to die?

Lisa found that three things helped her move from myth through the doorway into reality so she could accept Blackjack's death. Thinking and talking with understanding people about Blackjack's illness and approaching death helped. Each time she told the story, it felt a little more real to her. Writing about what Blackjack and she were going through also helped.

As she watched the illness weaken Blackjack's body, it became easier for her to accept how ill he really was. As medical attempts to reverse the illness were unsuccessful, she started to move toward accepting the reality that Blackjack was going to die.

TAKE ACTION. What are you doing to move beyond your myths and accept the reality of your pet's approaching death? Remember that it takes time to move beyond your myths.

CHAPTER 4

Facing the Reality

You will cross back and forth over the threshold between myth and reality numerous times, as you slowly move toward accepting reality. You hold on to your dying pet, briefly become aware of the reality of approaching death, and go back and continue your efforts to save her life. As you realize you have done everything you could do for your pet, and it isn't enough, you will decrease your unsuccessful attempts to keep your pet alive, and move through the door into reality. The process you are going through is:

Myth-Holding Onto Pet- Pain Circle ➡ Open Door into Reality

Bargaining With God. At some point in the euthanasia experience you will probably try to bargain with God to heal your pet. It might be before you cross the threshold into reality for the final time. When bargaining does not work, you will move ahead into reality.

How will I feel while crossing from myth into reality? You will feel stressed from your failed efforts to keep your pet alive. Physically you will feel exhausted, and won't feel like eating or sleeping. Emotionally you will feel frustrated, angry, and desperate as you realize you have done everything you could do, and it isn't enough. Time is running out.

As you move toward acceptance of your pet's death, you will reject your part in that death. However, you will never be able to forget that legally euthanasia is available to end suffering. Ambivalence, anger and guilt can tear you apart from this point on.

What actions can I take while crossing from myth into reality? You will continue last-ditch efforts to produce the desired outcome. And, when that fails, you may try to bargain with God to achieve the outcome you have been unable to achieve. You will consider euthanasia but quickly reject the idea.

CHAPTER 5

The Struggle To Let Go

Letting go is impossibly difficult. At first, you hold on tightly, thinking you will never be willing to let go. But the day will come when holding on becomes more painful than letting go.

I remember how I struggled against letting go. Ginny refused to take her medicine for the fourth time. Close to tears, I imagined throwing the medicine across the room. Without the medication, Ginny might die. Then I realized Ginny and I had different agendas. Mine was to prevent death. Her's was to die. It was time to redirect my energy to learning the lesson of letting go. In time, it became less painful to let go than to watch the suffering.

Letting go is a necessary step in making the euthanasia decision. The more tightly you hold on to your pet, and your need to keep her alive, the more frustrated you will feel as her condition worsens. Hanging on too tightly can affect you mentally through stress, physically through illnesses caused by stress, emotionally through feelings of anger, and spiritually through anger at God. Hanging on too tightly can also affect you financially through money you spend on expensive medical tests and treatments that can prolong your pet's suffering, rather than her life.

If you can come to the realization that hanging on is not helpful, and that some things are out of your control, you start a kind of metaphysical process in which you *let go*. As you let go, you turn the outcome over to the Universe or God, whatever your beliefs are. By letting go, you create an environment for a natural outcome, whatever that will be. Letting go will set you free from all the frustration you have been feeling. You can now use the energy you were using, as you tried to control the uncontrollable, in a more productive manner to care for yourself and your pet.

As you let go, tell yourself that your pet's cure was not meant to be. You can't understand why, but it just wasn't meant to be.

Giving Up and Letting Go. Is letting go the same as giving up? I think there is a *power difference* between the two. Giving up has a negative, weak, failure type of energy connected with it which lowers your self esteem.

Letting go is a deliberate choice you make. You could continue to try new ideas. You could continue to hang on longer. But you choose to let go. There is power involved in a letting-go decision that is not present in a giving-up decision.

TAKE ACTION. Can you view letting go as a positive, powerful choice you will make for yourself and your pet?

How long does it take to let go? Expect the process of letting go to take time. You will start to let go while you are in the myth-holding onto pet-pain circle. At this point, the letting go may be almost unconscious, with the loss of your pet being too painful to be considered for more than a brief time. After you cross through the doorway into reality, you will work more intensely on letting go.

As your dying pet becomes less capable of functioning and responding in a familiar way, the relationship changes. You will grieve the loss of your relationship with a healthy pet. And you will start to become more aware of letting go of your pet, and the relationship you two have shared.

You have two types of letting go to deal with: letting go of your pet's body, and letting go of your relationship with your living pet. After you let go of your pet's body and choose death, you will still have letting-go work to do regarding the relationship. The complexities of this relationship will leave emotional gaps in your life that need to be mourned.

When you let go enough so that you can choose death for your pet will be determined by a number of variables such as: your beliefs and values, the amount of suffering, your stress, and whether you feel you have done enough for your pet. Chapter 6 outlines these variables in more detail.

How will I feel while letting go? You will feel stress, anger at the loss of your pet's health and your pet's suffering, grief and anger at the loss of the relationship, and deep love for your pet.

The Emotional Work of Letting Go.

Letting go may be the hardest part for you, especially if you have a closer relationship with your pet than with any living person. Expect the letting-go work to continue after your pet's death.

Letting-go work will involve: 1) grieving for past life experiences, 2) grieving for unrealized future plans, 3) grieving for lost relationships, and 4) learning to accept life without your pet.

① **GRIEVING FOR PAST LIFE EXPERIENCES.** Experiences with your pet have been woven into your life history, maybe for many years. When you grieve the impending loss, you are also remembering and grieving for that part of your own life that is now behind you. As part of letting go of your pet, you will want to reminisce about the life events you two have shared.

TAKE ACTION. Take some time to remember where you were in your life when your pet entered it. What were your doing? What was life like for you then? Did you have any problems? What life experiences did you and your pet face together? What happy, funny, and sad memories do you have of your life with your pet?

② **GRIEVING FOR UNREALIZED FUTURE PLANS.** No matter how long your pet lives, she never lives long enough. You undoubtedly have made plans for your life with your pet far into the future. You need to grieve for what might have been.

TAKE ACTION. What plans did you have for yourself and your pet in the future? Take time to grieve the loss of the future with your pet.

③ **GRIEVING FOR LOST RELATIONSHIPS.** Pets often fill relationship roles that are missing in our lives. As part of letting go, you will need to grieve the loss of whatever relationship roles your pet was playing in your life.

Ideal parent. Sometimes your pet may seem to be an ideal parent. Such was the case for Tina, who had lived alone with her cat, Mouser, since her parents died. Tina viewed Mouser as a sort of ideal nurturing parent who gave her unconditional acceptance and love, was never too tired or too busy for her, and was supportive and validating.

Children who give meaning and purpose to life. Your pet's dependency on you creates a parent/child relationship between you and your pet. Since it is against the natural order for a child to die before the parents, this type of relationship creates special problems for you when your pet dies.

Joan missed her two children when they grew up and moved away to other parts of the United States. It was about that time that she brought two rabbits into her life to become her "children," as she called them. Interacting with and caring for her pets gave Joan a new purpose in life. Although these two "little girls" wouldn't grow up and leave, she became upset when she thought about outliving them.

Best friend. How often is a pet there for you when your human friends aren't? Jim was in an unhappy marriage which eventually ended in divorce. His dog, Mike, provided tremendous emotional support, and was always there to share his doubts and fears with as he moved out of this unhappy marriage.

Significant other. A pet has all the qualities of a perfect partner. When Audrey's dog, Jamie, was dying, she felt as though she was losing a partner because she had shared so much of her life with him. Jamie had been an almost perfect partner because he was so easy to please. He never complained about her cooking or argued with her the way her former husband had.

Your pet as a role model. Did you ever think of your pet as a role model? We often choose a human partner who has certain personality characteristics we would like to possess. For example, if you are the silent type, you might be attracted to a person who is a chatterbox. Likewise, you may find yourself attracted to an animal companion who embodies qualities you admire.

There are the physical qualities you might not possess but search for in a pet, such as the stereotype of the small man with the big, muscular watchdog. Personality qualities may be more subtle than the physical, but just as important, as we connect with "the right pet."

My dog, Annie, did what she wanted to, and was definitely *not* a "people pleaser." She had independence and self-assurance, the qualities I wanted to develop in myself. As soon as my back was turned, Annie climbed over the fence to chase rabbits or stole a piece of steak off my plate. She was not a good obedience candidate, but I didn't need that. I needed a role model who would challenge the rules, and Annie did, much to my delight.

Gina was struggling with trying to forgive people who had treated her abusively during childhood. She had been impressed by her dog's ability to love unconditionally and to forgive so easily – characteristics she was working on in herself.

If your relationship with your pet has this extension-of-personality component to it, you might feel as though you are considering putting to death a part of yourself when you think about euthanasia..

TAKE ACTION. Assess what life roles your pet has played for you. What personality characteristics that you would like to possess has your pet modeled for you? How successful have you been in acquiring those desired personality traits?

What actions can I take that will help me let go of my relationship with my pet? How do you let go of an emotionally intimate relationship with a pet who has been like a parent, child, best friend, significant other, or role model to you? We each have our own unique style of letting go. Usually we do something with or for our pet to create final happy memories, and to feel we have done everything we wanted to before the death. Planning favorite activities with your pet, taking lots of photos, videotaping his unique personality, talking with him, or writing a thank you letter to your pet are all ways to let go. Obtaining good medical care and home nursing will help you let go of a sick pet.

Following the death, you can pay tribute to your pet by various types of rituals and memorials. Funerals, the Candle Ceremony on the

Internet, and attending a pet loss support group are all letting-go rituals. Memorials that will help you let go include a grave marker, what you do with the ashes, or a charitable financial contribution in your pet's name. Chapter 19 discusses various types of pet memorials in more detail.

If you are having special problems letting go because you view your pet as a human companion, try Ted's approach of trying to see your pet as an animal instead of a person: Ted said he worked at seeing his dying cat, Aerial, as a cat instead of a person. As long as he viewed her as a child or best friend, he could not let go, and he could not make the euthanasia decision for her. Ted said that once he could see Aerial as a cat, he could let go of her enough to put her needs before his own, and choose euthanasia for her.

TO THINK ABOUT. Can you identify your unique style of letting go? Do you feel comfortable with your style, or would you rather let go in some other way?

④ LEARNING TO ACCEPT LIFE WITHOUT YOUR PET.

The final part of the letting-go process is getting used to thinking of your future life without your pet in it. The types of activities you two did together may have changed as your pet became feeble from age or illness. But your pet still probably took much of your time and energy, and was an emotional support to you.

Amy had trouble resolving her feelings about the loss of her dog, Scout, from her life. She knew that euthanasia had been the kindest death for Scout. What Amy could not accept was the loss of the relationship with Scout. Since she had retired, she had spent all her time with Scout training him for obedience class and shows. In fact, she had spent so much time with Scout that she had not developed any close human relationships.

After grieving alone for several months, Amy started attending a pet loss support group where she established some supportive relationships with people who accepted and understood her grief. In time, Amy felt ready for a new pet. As she channeled her energy into the relationships with her new pet and her new human friends, she realized that her grieving had diminished.

If, like Amy, you have been investing large amounts of time and energy in your relationship with your pet, you need to think about what you will do with your time and energy when your pet is no longer in your life. What new people, pets, and activities will you bring into your life to fill up your time?

Letting go of the intense emotional bond with your pet will touch you at a very deep level, and should not be minimized. Grieving for the relationship loss starts before your pet dies. It will continue after the death, until you accept your changed life without your pet. As difficult as it is to complete this step, you must let go before you can accept your loss and heal from your grief.

TAKE ACTION. Do you have people or other pets you can turn to for emotional support after you pet dies, or will you have to find new supports? Do you know how to find emotional support, if it is not already present in your life? See Chapter 17, Support Needs, for help with answers to these questions.

CHAPTER 6

How Will I Know
When It's Time?

Imagine a long line. At the beginning of the line your pet is young, vigorous and healthy. At the end of the line is your pet's death from natural causes. There is a point somewhere on the line when your pet starts to feel some physical discomfort, which will increase as he proceeds toward death. How do you go about deciding at what point on the time line you are ready to give up the fight, and ask your veterinarian to give your pet the "good death"? The answer to this question is very personal, and will be different for every pet owner. There is no one *right time* to make an euthanasia decision. If you don't make the decision today, you will have another opportunity to consider the situation, and make it tomorrow, if you want to do so. Just because you decided against euthanasia today, does not eliminate it as an option for tomorrow. One day you may say, as I did, that you could never choose death for your pet, and the next day you may decide to help your pet die.

The most important caution I can give is *not* to choose death for your pet only with the intellectual, reasoning side of your mind. You need to choose death with your heart. In other words, you must feel emotionally comfortable about your euthanasia decision.

Everyone has different thoughts about where on the time line they will make the euthanasia decision. Our culture doesn't handle aging or death very well. Going along with that line of thinking, is the idea that your pet will be less than his ideal, healthy self if you allow age or disease to take a toll on his body before death. You are asked if you want to remember your pet as old or ill? Euthanasia is given as the solution to this problem.

I call the above viewpoint "an intellectual argument." You might think you agree with it when your pet is young and healthy. But, when your pet is dying, your feelings will not allow you to think about euthanasia in such a detached, reasonable way.

The process of some bodily deterioration prior to the death gives both you and your dying pet time to prepare for the death. It doesn't mean you have to allow your pet to suffer intensely. But some indication of obvious illness will give both of you time to accept the reality of the approaching death, to let go, and to say your goodbyes.

You will not be so likely to feel guilty in the future if you witnessed some signs of your pet's failing health. Questions such as, "What if the veterinarian made the wrong diagnosis?" or "What if my pet wasn't really that ill?" can be answered if you did witness evidence of your pet's physical decline before you chose to help him die.

Donna was grieving and preparing herself for the euthanasia of her cat, Sam, one day when I stopped in at the bank where she worked. She knew Sam was suffering, but it was just so hard to let go. When I saw her after Sam's death, she showed me a picture her neighbor had taken the day before Sam's euthanasia. The photograph showed a thin, sick-looking cat when compared to earlier pictures showing Sam looking fat and sleek. Donna said that the photographs verified for her how very ill Sam had been at the time of his death, and reassured her that she had made the right decision.

Quality of Life Questions can help you decide whether it's time to seriously consider euthanasia for your pet. Such questions help you evaluate your pet's ability to live life with dignity and pain-free. Possible questions include:

- Is my pet in constant or extreme pain?
- Is my pet able to move by himself?
- Can my pet eat and drink by himself?
- Can my pet walk?
- Can my pet relieve himself?
- Can my pet interact with me and enjoy his surroundings?

TO THINK ABOUT. When do you think the euthanasia decision should be made? What are your beliefs and values? They will be behind whatever decision you make about pet euthanasia.

Formula For the Timing of the Euthanasia Decision

Many pet owners wonder why, at a specific time, they finally decided to help their pet die. If I had to devise a formula for the time that each of us chooses to make the euthanasia decision, I think it would be :

BV + S + SI + DE   =   Timing of the Euthanasia Decision.

The formula is: **BV**) your *beliefs* and *values*, plus **S**) the amount of *stress* you are already under at that time in your life, combined with **SI**) the *stress* the pet's *illness* puts you under, (including financial stress), and **DE**) whether you feel you have *done enough* for your pet.

The parts of this formula having to do with various types of *stress can hasten the rate* at which you choose death for your pet. The other two parts of the formula, having to do with your *beliefs and values, and doing enough for your pet*, can delay, sometimes indefinitely, your euthanasia decision for your pet. Let's consider how the various parts of this formula can affect the timing of euthanasia.

① **BELIEFS AND VALUES.** Your beliefs and values help you answer questions such as:

1) *How do you react to failing health in someone you love?*
2) *How low a quality of life can you tolerate in someone you love?*
3) *How long can you watch someone you love suffer?*
4) *Can you justify medical procedures that increase suffering for your pet in order to prolong life for a limited period of time?*
5) *How much money are you willing to spend to prolong your pet's life for an unknown, but possibly short, period of time?*
6) *What kinds of things do you want to do for/with your pet so you will feel you have done enough and can let go of your pet?*
7) *How do you feel about choosing death for your pet?*

Your answers to these seven questions will enter into your decision about when to choose euthanasia for your pet. You may not know the answers to these questions when you start this experience, but you will by the time your pet dies.

Joe was a military man whose personal philosophy about life and death was that he would rather be in pain and alive than dead. Whenever he was in severe pain, he told himself, "At least I'm still alive, and that is all that counts." Therefore, early in his cat's illness, he did not think suffering was a reason to end Bugle's life. Since Joe's sister felt differently, Joe gave permission for his sister to make arrangements for Bugle to be euthanized when her pain became severe.

The most difficult part of the euthanasia decision for Anne concerned her values that were opposed to taking life. She had grown up in a farming community where chickens routinely were beheaded on the chopping block for Sunday dinner. Lambs and pigs were butchered for meat. Everyone, except Anne, seemed to take the killing in stride. The animals gave Anne lots of emotional support, and she felt pain when one of her friends was killed. She vowed she would never kill. Choosing death for an animal, even a dying animal, was going against Anne's values, and it delayed her euthanasia decision.

Your Values and Your Profession. *In All Things Wise and Wonderful*, James Herriot said that he hated doing euthanasia, even though he knew it was painless. But he found comfort in the fact that the final thing the animals experienced was hearing a "a friendly voice" and feeling "the touch of a gentle hand."

There are some veterinarians and technicians who find it upsetting to euthanize an animal when there is medical treatment that could cure the pet's condition, or when an adoptive home could be found. What should you do if your values conflict with the pet owner's values? Should you go against your values and help a pet die unnecessarily as part of your work?

It is possible that, if the professional refuses to help their pet die, the pet owner may just go to another veterinarian, or may abandon the pet so it becomes a stray, or even kill the animal in an inhumane way. If you know the pet could suffer a worse fate, if you don't provide humane euthanasia, how would you respond to the euthanasia request?

Consider all the factors involved. Think long and hard about what your values are in regard to this dilemma.

You need to be able to justify the euthanasia to yourself. If you routinely go against you values and do euthanasias you can't justify to yourself, it could damage your self esteem, eventually lead to burn-out, and could cause you to leave your profession.

TO THINK ABOUT. **Which of your beliefs or values might interfere with choosing death for your pet?**

② **AMOUNT OF STRESS IN YOUR LIFE.** I believe that the current level of stress in your life has a major influence on how quickly you let go and choose death for your pet. What type of stress is present in your life apart from the stress of an ill pet? Existing problems such as: your own poor health, several ill pets, a job loss or change, a demanding job, a divorce, a death, an aged parent, a move, or a child leaving home — all are examples of additional stressful problems that might exist in your life in conjunction with your pet's illness.

Each person has his own maximum stress level. When you reach your maximum stress level, you will not be able to tolerate any additional stress without it seriously affecting your mental and physical health.

Betsy nursed her dying dog, Ember, until her senile father-in-law moved in with the family. The increased load of stress from her in-law, combined with the demands of caring for a very ill pet, led Betsy to make the euthanasia decision for Ember. The intensity of Betsy's stress level was the key to when she decided on euthanasia. It was not simply the degree of Ember's suffering.

TAKE ACTION. **Identify what life problems are contributing to your stress at this time.**

③ **THE STRESS YOUR PET'S ILLNESS PUTS YOU UNDER.** It is stressful to care for an ill and dying pet. It takes a lot of time and patience to give medications to an unwilling pet, to hand feed, clean up after, and carry a dying pet around. If you were already under some type of life stress when your animal became ill, nursing him will surely increase your stress, and could force you to seriously consider death for your pet.

Travel away from home. The constant care ties you down so you can't go far from home. What if your job demands you be away from home a great deal? How will you care for your dying pet? What if your pet is ill or dying, and your vacation time comes around? If you can't be present to care for your pet, it is difficult to find someone else to take over the nursing of a dying pet. Leaving your pet without adequate care would increase her suffering. These difficult dilemmas may lead to an appropriate euthanasia decision for your pet.

Financial stress. The issue of financial stress is significant when you weigh the cost of financial care for a dying pet. Where do you set the limit for how much to spend on medical bills? Do you use your vacation money for your pet's bills? Do you use your child's college tuition money? Where do you draw the line? Take time to review the questions about money in Chapter 13.

The effect on other pets. How will all the time involved in caring for your dying pet impact your other pets? Chances are, they will start to feel somewhat neglected. Is this fair to them?

Stress from specific physical symptoms. Sometimes a specific symptom of a pet's deteriorating health will increase your stress level to the point where you say,"The value of prolonging my pet's life for a short time is not worth the stress I am going through watching him exhibit this physical symptom."

Brad decided to euthanize his elderly dog, Pepper, the day Pepper went totally blind and started bumping into the furniture. Pepper did not appear to be in any physical pain, but was so unlike his former confident self that Brad could not handle his stress at seeing his dog so changed.

Why no one else can make the euthanasia decision for you. Like Brad, I think that many of us have a stressful reaction to a specific physical symptom. This symptom may decrease the quality of life. It may or may not cause suffering or pain for your pet. For one person, the symptom might be his pet's deafness. For another, it might be blindness, or a seizure, or incontinence, or inability to walk. That is why no one else can make the euthanasia decision for you. Everyone is stressed by different symptoms.

When someone tells you they think you should euthanize your pet, they are telling you they could not live with your pet's particular symptom. You might think, "Why I could have tolerated that problem," or "I could *never* put up with that problem," as you hear people talk about the various health problems of their pets. Some decide to end a pet's life when it goes blind or deaf. Others tell of pets who seem to be alert and enjoying life to some extent, even though blind and deaf. How do you react to a pet who is incontinent, has pain when walking, or has trouble eating?

TO THINK ABOUT. *Which symptoms or health problems would you be able or not be able to deal with?*

Similar owner-pet illnesses. When the pet owner and the pet have the same medical problem, it will compound the stress the owner experiences.

Marie felt guilty when she chose death for her Dachshund, Schultzie, who suffered from the same spinal condition she had. Although she had alleviated her own spinal problem with surgery, she could not afford such surgery for Schultzie. However, since she knew from personal experience how painful that spinal problem was, she was glad she could spare Schultzie that suffering.

On the positive side, talking about your pet's illness and death gives you an opportunity to express your feelings about your own similar illness and/or approaching death in a way that you might not have done otherwise.

TAKE ACTION. *Identify the ways your pet's illness has added stress to your life. How well are you handling the stress? Refer to Chapter 17 for suggestions on how to handle stress.*

④ **DOING ENOUGH BEFORE LETTING GO.** What else do you want to do for your pet in order to feel you have done enough before letting go?

Favorite activities.   You might plan special, favorite activities with their pet, or give special foods or grooming to help you feel you have done enough so you can let go.

Intensive care by owner. You might find it comforting to nurse your dying pet as a way of letting go.

Medical treatment. You might want to take advantage of all available medical treatment to feel you have done enough.

May took her parakeet, Aqua, to a special bird veterinarian to make sure she had the most advanced medical care. That was her way of making sure she had done enough before she let go.

Sometimes a pet will die during, or as a result of, medical treatment. Before agreeing to medical treatment, be prepared to accept your pet's death if that is the outcome of medical treatment. *It complicates your grief if what you did to make sure you did enough for your pet, ends up causing your pet's premature death.*

Pressure From the Legality of Euthanasia Leads to Guilt.
Did I Do It Soon Enough? You know you have an obligation and responsibility to care for your pet throughout his life, and to arrange a peaceful death at the end of life. When it comes to that final responsibility, euthanasia is a legal option for animals. Because it *is* an option, you may feel pressure from others, or even yourself, to choose euthanasia for a dying animal friend, before you are truly ready to choose it. Before the death, you may feel guilty for not choosing euthanasia whenever someone points out to you that you pet is very ill. After the euthanasia, many people feel guilty because they didn't do it earlier.

Mel told me he had not felt guilty about choosing euthanasia for his elderly, dying dog, Brady. But choosing euthanasia for Nugget, a young dog dying of cancer who was still mentally alert, was very difficult. Nugget was so alert that Mel did not realize how much she was suffering. When he recognized that she was in pain, he made euthanasia arrangements. But to this day he still wonders, "Did I do it soon enough?"

To this question I reply, *"You did it when you felt emotionally ready to do it."*

If you find yourself asking the question: "Did I do it soon enough?" review the emotional work involved in the seven steps of the euthanasia experience, listed in Chapter 2, to remind yourself of why it takes so much time to make the euthanasia decision. Did you take time to go through the necessary emotional steps before you chose death for your pet? *You must be psychologically ready before you can feel comfortable with the euthanasia decision.*

If, for some reason, you chose euthanasia too quickly, without taking enough time to feel ready, you may feel guilty. Then you will have to identify what emotional work you have to complete to overcome your guilt. Perhaps you have to finish letting go of the relationship, or convince yourself that you chose death because of your love for your pet. Refer to the discussion on guilt in Chapter 16.

GUIDELINES FOR CHOOSING EUTHANASIA

Do not choose euthanasia with your head alone because it makes sense.

Do not choose euthanasia to please someone else.

Do not choose euthanasia because you feel guilty for not choosing it.

When you have done what you need to do to end your relationship with your living pet . . . .

Then you can choose euthanasia with your heart,

Because you feel it is the best kind of death for your pet,

When your pet is at the end of his life.

TO THINK ABOUT. If you choose death for your pet with love in your heart, after doing everything you can do, you decrease the chances of feeling guilty about the euthanasia. You have painlessly released your pet from a worn-out body and further suffering.
YOU ARE INNOCENT.

CHAPTER 7

Emotional Blocks to Euthanasia

Before you can accept your part in your pet's death, you have to undergo a transition in your feelings from horror and despair at the thought of ending the life of a loved one, to a recognition that arranging a quick, painless death is the final, most loving gift you can give your pet. Before this shift in your thinking can take place, you need to deal with any emotional blocks that could keep you from choosing death for your pet when the time comes. Possible emotional blocks include:

- Your anxiety about death
- Your feelings about killing, and your part in euthanasia
- Traumatic memories of previous euthanasias
- The abuse-of-power issue
- Difficulty in letting go of the relationship with your pet

Your emotional blocks make choosing euthanasia for your pet a traumatic life event. Each issue by itself is enough to trigger a painful life crisis, and dealing with several of these matters simultaneously can feel overwhelming. A diagram of what you are going through would look like this:

Suffering Pet ▐ Emotional Blocks ▐ Legal Euthanasia

Your love for your pet, and seeing euthanasia as a loving way to end your pet's suffering, are what will help you eventually move beyond your emotional blocks.

As we look at each of the emotional blocks, try to determine which blocks are creating problems for you. In the following sections, any strong emotional reactions will warn you about a sensitive issue that may interfere with your ability to handle your pet's death.

Your Feelings About Death

Death is a natural life experience. But it does not feel natural to most people. It feels terrifying. Most of our lives we use various strategies to avoid our anxiety about death. Terms like "pass away" or "put to sleep" help us avoid even saying the dreaded word "death." But, when you can no longer avoid a confrontation with death, how do you deal with your death anxiety?

Start by facing death directly. Go into your memory. How much experience have you had with death and dying? Have you ever gone through the death experience with someone you love? If so, think back to that time. Remember how important and precious those final days or moments were. Final thoughts and actions in a relationship leave an indelible impression, and you want them to feel right. If there were moments in that death experience you feel uncomfortable about, how would you like to do things differently this time? With euthanasia, you have control over how, when, and where the death happens.

If you have never gone through the death experience with someone you cared for deeply, you may not know what feelings to expect as you face this unknown experience. Common feelings you can expect include: intense anxiety, fear, anger, sadness, and guilt. Chapter 16 will help you handle each of these distressing feelings.

If you have had close people or pets die in the past, you may still have grief to express regarding the loss of these other relationships. Such unexpressed grief will intensify your present grief because now you have feelings about multiple losses to deal with at the same time.

Deaths that you may still have grief feelings about could include: abortions, miscarriages, stillbirths, parents, parent substitutes, siblings, other relatives, friends, or favorite pets. Premature or sudden deaths often have intense long-term grief feelings connected with them, especially if you feel guilty, or blame yourself for the death.

As part of thinking about death, and your involvement in your pet's death, you might want to take time to review your previous experiences with death by writing down the answers to the following questions:

Previous Deaths

Has anyone (human or pet) you loved died?
Was the death sudden, or was there an extended illness?
What was that experience like for you?
Were you there at the time of death? Do you wish you had been?
Did you express your feelings about the death? How did you do that?
What were your needs? Did others respond to your needs?
Do you feel guilty, in any way, about that death?
How long did you grieve?
Did your parents cry when someone died?

Feelings About Death Today

How do you feel about death today?
What helps you the most when you are grieving?

Feelings About Grieving the Death of a Pet

How were pet deaths treated in your family when you were a child?
Did your parents ever hide a pet's death from you?
Did you have funerals for deceased pets?
Do you think it is okay to grieve the death of a pet? Or, are you ashamed of your feelings of grief over the death of a pet?
Has anyone ever said critical things to you about grieving the death of a pet? If so, what? What did you say/do?
Can you talk to others about your feelings concerning pet death?

Your Philosophy of Life and Death

What is your philosophy of life and death?
What do you think happens after death?
Do you think there is a "life after death" for pets?

TAKE ACTION. Your answers to these questions will help you start thinking about death and grief, and how involved you want to be in your pet's death. Which questions stirred up feelings? Talking and writing about your feelings will help. Do you think you need to get some help for yourself in the form of counseling or a support group as you face the death of your pet?

Your Feelings About Euthanasia Killing

We live in a society that does not approve of a planned death for humans. Abortion, murder, suicide, or human euthanasia are not acceptable. And, yet, you are encouraged to put your pet "out of his misery," and not feel too upset about it.

Cynthia's 12-year-old cat, Mozart, was slowly declining from a serious heart condition. Cynthia's friend asked her whether she had thought about "putting Mozart out of his misery." When Cynthia thought of killing Mozart, she felt nauseated with anxiety and fear. Next, she felt ashamed of getting so upset. So she tried to minimize her feelings. She told himself that logically euthanasia would be the right thing to do because it would end Mozart's' suffering. Cynthia had used logic to push her feelings back down inside. Her body responded to this coverup of feelings by giving her a headache and an upset stomach.

Most of us would react the way Cynthia did. Choosing death for the companion we have one of our closest emotional bonds with can feel more like murder rather than an act of mercy. *The euthanasia decision comes from love, not cruelty or an intention to do harm.* But it may take your feelings time to come to that realization. Start out by accepting your feelings. Don't push them away, or cover them up with logic because you are ashamed of them. Talk about your feelings to people who understand. Throughout this chapter, we will discuss how your mindset regarding killing needs to change before you can accept euthanasia killing as a way to lovingly end suffering.

Are euthanasia and assisted dying the same as killing?

Is euthanasia really killing, or is it assisted dying? Killing involves the intention to do harm to another. It involves ending another's life against their will and without their consent. Assisted dying is a compassionate act to help a pet who is suffering as he approaches physical death. The intent of euthanasia is closer to the definition of assisted dying than the definition of killing.

However, assisted dying usually implies the consent of the one who is dying. This is where there is lots of room for confusion and guilty feelings in connection with pet euthanasia. Although you want to humanely assist your pet in dying, it can feel like killing because of the lack of verbal communication. How can an animal communicate her consent to you? How can you communicate to your pet your intent to help, and not do harm?

Communicate With Your Pet About Euthanasia. Try talking to your pet about his situation and your concerns about whether to choose euthanasia for him. Even though he can't verbally tell you what he wants, there is much nonverbal communication that takes place between you and your pet.

Hold or touch your pet, look into his eyes to get his attention, and tell him how you feel about what he is going through. Explain what you are feeling about losing him. Talk to him about all you have done to avoid euthanasia as long as possible. Explain that medical treatment might be able to prolong his life, and possibly his suffering, for a long time. Ask your pet how he feels about your making arrangements to end his suffering and release him from his ill or infirm body. Tell him you want to make the best decision for him – the decision he would make for himself, if he could.

Most pets are intuitive, and, if they aren't too ill, will respond to what you are saying to them. Clear your mind and see what feelings you can pick up from your pet about what he/she would like to have happen in the matter of life and death.

A Caution. Communicating with your pet is not a way to get out of making the euthanasia decision. *You are still the one who will have to make the final decision.* But the feeling that you have talked to your pet about the situation, and that your pet understands and is in agreement with your decision, can go a long way towards helping you feel that a euthanasia decision is assisted dying rather than killing.

Questions About Euthanasia, Assisted Dying, and Killing. Think about how you would answer the following questions:

◆ *What thoughts and feelings do you associate with killing? Do you associate anger, violence, or cruelty with killing?*

♦ *What thoughts and feelings do you associate with assisted dying or euthanasia? Have you had any experience with euthanasia in your life? If so, how did you feel about it?*

♦ *Can you view pet euthanasia as assisted dying rather than killing? Can you connect the feeling of love with euthanasia?*

Memories of Previous Events

If you pull a plant out of the ground, it's impossible to avoid pulling up other growing plants whose roots are entwined with the plant you are disturbing. Likewise, the euthanasia decision will touch and stir up both painful and positive memories and feelings. Difficult memories may include such things as previous deaths, euthanasias, relationship losses, or abuses of power. Such upsetting memories will complicate the euthanasia experience, and can prolong your grief. I hope you will also touch some positive, powerful memories that will give you strength at this time.

Previous Negative Euthanasia Experiences. Many people have had a previous negative experience with euthanasia.

George, aged 78, still remembers that day 65 years ago when he lost his best friend, a Collie named Laddie. George and Laddie had grown up together and were inseparable. But Laddie was growing old and deaf. He was only trying to protect himself when the hyperactive little boy from down the street surprised him by pulling his tail. Laddie didn't bite the child, but he did snap at him.

George's parents did not tell him they had decided that it was best to end Laddie's life. He still remembers how empty he felt inside when his father handed him Laddie's collar and told him Laddie was dead. He grieved for years, and, although his parents told him he could have any dog he wanted, George never could get interested in another dog. Sixty-five years later, he still feels sad that he wasn't able to say goodbye and comfort Laddie before he died.

Secretive euthanasias of childhood pets can be a profoundly upsetting experience for a child. The need to involve a child in the euthanasia of his pet is more fully discussed in Chapter 10.

If you had such a negative euthanasia experience in your childhood, what effect is that early experience having on your current euthanasia experience/decision? Answer the following questions to determine how the previous experience is affecting you today.

Recalling Earlier Euthanasia Experiences.

Remember the pet involved. What did that pet mean to you? What relationship did you have with that pet? What adult authority figures were involved in the euthanasia of your pet? How was the decision made to end your pet's life? Who made that decision? Did you have a say in what happened to end your pet's life? Did you have a chance to say goodbye to your pet? What do you wish had been done differently back then? How did you feel, at the time, about your pet's death? How do you feel today?

I have known people who were able to draw on a negative childhood pet euthanasia experience to plan a more positive euthanasia experience for their present-day pet. This time *they* made the decisions. As they did things the way they wanted them, they sort of "made up" for the damaging childhood experience.

Mike decided on euthanasia for his elderly cat friend, Tiger, who was slowly dying. Mike had gone through a terrible euthanasia experience in childhood when his sick cat, his only confidant in a severely dysfunctional family, was ripped from his arms and taken to the veterinarian to be euthanized. It's no wonder that even the thought of euthanasia paralyzed Mike with fear.

Mike took several months to make the decision, and carefully planned the details of the euthanasia. He held Tiger and talked to him as the injection was given. As Tiger's body relaxed, Mike suddenly realized how much pain Tiger had been enduring in recent months. Next, Mike felt his own terror about the finality of the euthanasia, and the love it took to let go of Tiger. A close, loving, spiritual feeling followed, as Mike felt Tiger's life and spirit leave his body. Mike said he felt at peace with this euthanasia experience because this time he had control over what happened. Somehow, it felt like a corrective emotional experience to him.

Euthanasia And The Abuse of Power Issue

It is rare to get through childhood without having at least one adult abuse the power they have over you. Abuse of power can take many forms: mental, emotional, physical, or sexual. It can be occasional or frequent. It can come from family members, teachers, employers, or other persons outside the family. The impact that the abuse of power left on you is determined by who the abuser was, how frequently the power was abused, and whether you were able to tell someone and stop the abuse.

Many pet owners have formed such an emotionally close trusting relationship with their pet because they have trouble trusting people. And, frequently, that unwillingness to trust people goes back to some form of power abuse in childhood. Even if you do trust people, and didn't have any form of serious abuse in childhood, you may have had at least one person in your adult life, such as an employer, abuse whatever power they had over you. If that is true, you will be sensitive to the abuse-of-power issue.

Remember the metaphor of the plant whose roots are entangled under the ground with the roots of various other plants? The abuse-of-power issue is a major problem that is stirred up for many people as they consider choosing death for their pet. Those who experienced serious power abuses during childhood are deeply affected by this issue.

If you were abused early in life, you easily feel another's pain. You identify with the victim role because you know what it feels like to be victimized. As you consider euthanasia, in your mind your pet becomes the victim, and you become the abuser. But you know how the victim feels. So, the logical thing for you to do is to rescue the victim and stop the abuse. In this case, the rescue would involve not choosing death for your pet.

If we diagramed the feelings, it would look like this:

Pet = Victim to be killed   Owner Choosing Death = Abuser

Rescue by Not Performing Euthanasia

However, a further dilemma arises if you can see that your pet is suffering and in pain. Euthanasia is the only way to rescue your pet from his pain. Your mind will have to view euthanasia as a kind of rescue, and not a form of abuse, in order for you to end your pet's life without feeling as though you are abusing your power. You will need to feel that, in using your power to give your pet a good death, you are, in fact, rescuing your pet from suffering.

Diagramed out, the picture would look like this:

Pet = Suffering Victim   Illness = Abuser

Rescue   by   Euthanasia

If you can take this view of euthanasia, you will have broken a connection in your mind between killing and abuse of power. You will no longer be connecting euthanasia killing with an *abuse of your power*. You will now mentally be connecting euthanasia with a *positive use of your power* to end your pet's suffering.

The diagram would look like this:

First Mental Connection: Euthanasia = Abuse of Power

**New Connection: Euthanasia = Using Power Positively
to End Suffering and to Rescue**

If you think your uncomfortable feelings about euthanasia may be triggered by past power abuses in your life, consider the following questions:

+ *Did something happen to you when you were a child that was, or may have been, abusive? What was it?*
+ *What feelings do you still have about that childhood abusive experience?*
+ *Do you still feel like a victim?*
+ *Do you identify with people or animals who appear to be victims?*
+ *Are you inclined to rescue victims (animals or people)?*

◆   *What childhood issues are present for you when you consider the euthanasia decision?*
◆   *Are there times, when you are upset about ending your pet's life, that you feel younger than your present age?*
◆   *If so, how old do you feel?*

Chances are, your upset feelings about this euthanasia decision are related to unresolved feeling about an abusive experience that happened to you when you were the age you just stated. The intensity of the feelings that are coming up for you now will let you know how seriously that abuse in the past impacted your life.

Do your answers to these questions indicate you still have some unresolved strong feelings about abusive authority figures and victims that are influencing your decision about euthanasia?

Euthanasia and Memories of Rejecting Parents.   Unresolved parent/child issues, in which your parent acted in a rejecting/neglectful way to you during childhood, may be stirred up during a euthanasia experience. Examples of this would be children who feel they were neglected by parents for a number of reasons: alcoholism, parental mental illness, or a difficult divorce. Also, adopted children frequently feel they were rejected by the birth parent who surrendered them for adoption.

The decision to choose death for a pet could feel like a type of neglect or rejection, with the pet playing the role of the neglected or rejected child, and the pet's owner playing the role of the neglectful/rejecting parent.

Past unresolved issues such as these can complicate or delay euthanasia planning. If talking with supportive friends or writing about your feelings doesn't help enough, you might decide to talk with a professional counselor. A counselor can help you identify, understand, and resolve feelings about childhood power abuses or rejections so that you can avoid long-term guilt about your part in choosing death for your pet.

At first, Dennis didn't make the connection between the guilt stirred up by the euthanasia of his horse, Gambit, and his early childhood history. With the help of a counselor, Dennis identified how a rejecting alcoholic parent, and a difficult divorce between his parents had left him feeling very protective of anyone he perceived to be rejected as he had been. Dennis' intense guilt occurred because he viewed euthanasia as a form of rejection rather than a release from suffering. After talking and writing about his feelings over a period of time, Dennis came to perceive the choice of euthanasia for Gambit as an act of love rather than a rejection.

Another complicating memory is a connection between a pet euthanasia decision and a decision to shut off human life-support, or give large amounts of pain-killers that might hasten a suffering family member's death.

Frank was having a difficult time dealing with his feelings about his mother's approaching death, especially regarding the decision to shut off her life support. The rest of the family were in favor of this, but Frank was not. Suddenly he thought of the terrible struggle he had gone through the previous year with his terminally ill puppy. He finally had euthanized the pup when the veterinarian could do nothing further. He felt certain his unresolved feelings about the pet euthanasia were contributing to his upset about shutting off his mother's life support.

TAKE ACTION. Are difficult memories interfering with your decision about choosing death for your pet? If so, what do you plan to do about it?

Importance of Identifying Your Emotional Blocks

If this is your first experience with death, your feelings about death might be what stir up the most upsetting feelings. If this is a pet who is giving you lots of emotional support, you will have an especially difficult time letting go of the relationship. Or you may not want any part of euthanasia, if you view it as murder. Memories of childhood pet euthanasias or power abuses may be triggered by this euthanasia experience. There is a good chance you will have problems dealing with one or more of these life events.

During my euthanasia experience, whenever I experienced sadness, fear or anger, I found it helpful to ask whether the feeling was connected with my reaction to: 1) killing, 2) death, 3) childhood memories, or 4) the loss of my relationship with Ginny. It gave me a sense of control to sort out what part of the experience was triggering which feeling. The feeling of having some control is so helpful in getting through the euthanasia experience.

TAKE ACTION. Whenever you have a feeling, such as sadness or anger, ask yourself what part of the experience is triggering that feeling. Is death, killing, relationship loss, or difficult memories bringing up your feeling?

Identifying which part of the experience was causing a feeling helped me know what issue I was having the most trouble dealing with. When I no longer got upset feelings about one of the issues, I knew I had resolved my feelings about that matter. Before I made the euthanasia decision, I had intense feelings about death and killing. After making the euthanasia decision, I realized I had moved beyond most of my feelings about death and killing. The sadness I felt during Ginny's euthanasia was primarily connected with the loss of Ginny from my life.

It is possible to become stuck in your feelings about one or more of these four matters so that you can't resolve your feelings about the euthanasia experience. If you feel you are "stuck" in your feelings, try to identify which issue you can't get beyond.

TAKE ACTION. If you feel stuck, write down the thoughts that are going through your mind about that issue. Read what you have written, and look for clues about what is giving you trouble resolving the matter. What action could you take to move beyond where you seem to be stuck?

CHAPTER 8

Choosing Death for Your Pet

A Final Bargaining With God. You know it is time to make the dreaded decision. Your pet is suffering, or has lost all capacity to enjoy life. Heart racing with dread, you pick up the phone to call the veterinarian and schedule the euthanasia. But, wait! Maybe you should try to bargain with God one last time. In desperation you beg for a miracle that will take away this terrible responsibility from you. If your pet would just have a heart attack, you wouldn't have to be involved in the death. But your pet's heart doesn't stop, and you realize that God will work through you to end your pet's life. Tearfully you pick up the phone and call your veterinarian.

How will I feel as I choose death for my pet? The most common feelings include: fear regarding death and killing, anger at having to make the decision, and stress while making the decision. After the decision is made, you may have a deep feeling of love that comes from putting someone else's needs ahead of your own. Feelings of uncertainty and guilt may lessen or disappear. You will feel that you are making, or have made, the right decision. You will feel relief, and at peace that you chose a painless way of death to end your pet's suffering. These feelings have occurred for some people at the time of the euthanasia decision, for others when they were present at the moment of their pet's death, and for others sometime after the death.

At the time of the euthanasia, you may feel anxious or fearful. You will feel overwhelming sadness, and deep love for your pet. I found that being present at the moment of death (what I believe to be the departure of the spirit or soul from the body), was as emotionally awesome an experience as being present at a birth.

Recognition of Physical Suffering. This usually precedes the euthanasia decision. However, there are times when your mind won't recognize a pet's suffering because you are not ready to deal with that knowledge.

Jan's veterinarian noticed that Jan did not wonder whether her dying cat, Abigail, was feeling pain. Jan wasn't asking about pain because she was not yet ready to choose euthanasia, which would have been the way to go if she knew her pet was suffering.

I have had many pet owners tell me of experiencing a moment when they suddenly looked at their dying pet with " new eyes," and saw the true deterioration of their pet's body, as if for the first time. This usually happens around the time of the euthanasia decision, maybe just before, or just after.

Jim said, that right before he made the euthanasia decision, he suddenly realized, for the first time, how thin and terribly ill his cancer-stricken dog, Rip, looked. Rip must have been that thin for weeks, but he had never allowed himself to see it. As soon as he saw his dog's true suffering, he immediately phoned his veterinarian to arrange euthanasia.

It seems your conscious mind prevents you from seeing the bodily deterioration until around the time you are ready to take action. Even if your veterinarian points out the suffering, you may not be able to acknowledge your pet's suffering to yourself until you are ready to let go.

Guilt may accompany your observation of you pet's suffering, and you may wonder why you waited so long. The answer to the question of why you wait "so long" is that you need to address the necessary emotional work before you are ready to let go and choose euthanasia for your pet. If our pets could talk, I think they would tell us they understand how difficult it is for us to face reality, let go, and make this life and death decision.

Sudden Euthanasia Decisions. Many pet owners worry because they appear to make their euthanasia decision suddenly, almost impulsively, after a period of time when they could not seem to act. However, the decision comes at the end of an emotional and logical working through of the issues. It may seem impulsive. But it isn't.

Rehearsal for Euthanasia. The first time your veterinarian mentions the option of euthanasia, your mind starts preparing you to make the euthanasia decision, as you briefly picture what it would be like to euthanize your pet. Later, when you move from your myths into reality, euthanasia will always be in the logical part of your mind as an option, even though you still emotionally reject it. During this time, you might think or talk to others about details regarding euthanasia, such as: who would drive you to the veterinarian's, or what you would do if your pet needed euthanasia in the middle of the night, or what happens during euthanasia. I call that mental preparation "rehearsal for euthanasia." The rehearsal helps prepare you for the emotional acceptance of euthanasia, when it becomes necessary.

Planning When and Where the Euthanasia Will Take Place. After choosing euthanasia for your pet, you need to decide when it will be done. One option is to schedule it during your veterinarian's regular office hours. The other option is to wait until you know your pet is suffering or close to dying. This might happen at an inconvenient time (middle of the night or weekend) when your regular veterinarian's office is closed. In such a case, unless your regular veterinarian had agreed to be on call for an emergency euthanasia, you may end up at an emergency veterinary clinic with an unknown veterinarian doing the euthanasia.

You, also, need to plan where the euthanasia will take place. The most common options are the veterinarian's office or your home. Talk to your veterinarian, and think about what feels the most comfortable for you and your pet.

What actions can I take before and after choosing euthanasia?

❖ Know that you have done everything you wanted to do for your pet prior to choosing death for your pet.

❖ Put your pet's well-being ahead of your own wishes not to be involved in his death.

❖ Plan where and when the euthanasia will take place. When you talk to your veterinarian about helping your pet die peacefully, ask your vet to verify that your pet's medical condition is, indeed, terminal. If you need reassurance from your veterinarian that euthanasia is a swift, painless leaving of life, ask for that.

❖   Talk to your pet about what you have asked your veterinarian to do, and why you did so. Say goodbye to your pet. Pets do not appear to fear death, but they don't like to leave you. So, reassure your pet that you will be sad, but you will be okay.

❖   Decide whether you want to be present to comfort your pet during the euthanasia.

❖   Make arrangements to pay for the euthanasia *before* the euthanasia, if possible.

❖   Make final arrangements for your pet's body.

TAKE ACTION. Identify where you are in facing the realities, in letting go, and in choosing death for your pet. Do you feel you are moving ahead? If not, where are you stuck?

Choosing Death for Ginny

My euthanasia experience started before dinner one evening in early November. Suddenly my 14-year-old dog, Ginny, went into a seizure. She looked like she was dying. Ginny, who had danced over the rocks on Monhegan Island like a mountain goat, who had pulled out the toothpicks marking David's newly planted seed flats, who loved peach shortcake with vanilla ice cream, and who was the mother of my first champion, little Ginny was dying – except she didn't.

Medication stopped the seizures, but her mind was clouded for days. While I hoped she would recover completely and be like her former self, people started hinting that euthanasia would be a kindness. With a sick feeling in my stomach, I tried to picture what it would be like to help Ginny die, and decided I could never do it. I really didn't think she was going to die. But, if she didn't get better, I decided to just let her die naturally, hopefully, in her sleep.

The option of euthanasia would not leave my thoughts. As the months went by, Ginny had some good days, but her quality of life was gradually deteriorating. Sometimes I felt guilty for not choosing euthanasia instead of waiting for a natural death. I thought about which veterinarian was close by if Ginny suddenly went into medical crisis, and I had to help her die.

Ginny needed so much special care, and I gave it to her. When she wouldn't eat, I even hand-fed her. But the stress of this intense care was starting to wear me down. There were days I felt like fighting for Ginny's life, and days I felt like giving up – especially when she wouldn't take her medication. Sometimes I felt like throwing the medication across the room. But I didn't throw the medication, and I didn't give up. I wasn't ready to let go yet.

One day Ginny seemed especially weak. As my stress level rose, I wondered how much more I could take. I was almost ready to let go. I phoned the veterinarian hoping he would make my decision for me by saying she was too ill, and euthanasia was the only answer. But I learned he wouldn't be in for two days.

Suddenly I felt so much relief, and was glad he wasn't in. I would not have to help Ginny die that day. Ginny seemed better that night, and I was glad she was still alive. I felt guilty for making the phone call, and was sure I would not have to choose euthanasia. I prayed she would just get weaker, and die by herself.

Ginny's seizure medication stopped working late the next night. She started having seizures. As my stress level skyrocketed, my ambivalence about euthanasia ended abruptly. Ginny was suffering. I had done everything I could do for her. I had to let go and choose death for Ginny.

Dramatically, my whole attitude toward euthanasia changed. For the first time, I was glad euthanasia was legally available. Releasing Ginny from her worn-out body was most loving gift I could give her now. I told Ginny, and felt she somehow understood.

When I wondered how guilty I would feel for choosing death for Ginny, the words, "You are innocent" popped into my mind. I realized ending life with euthanasia was not murder. Euthanasia was an act of mercy done with love. When I focused on feeling the love, my guilt diminished. I felt the overwhelming sadness of loss, but not guilt.

The morning she was to die, Ginny was very groggy after the series of seizures. She looked like a little puppy as I carried her wrapped up in a pink blanket into Dr. Harvey's office.

When I saw a girl behind the counter hand-feeding a newborn puppy, I remembered what a good mother Ginny had been. The past and the present, beginnings and endings, joy of birth and sadness of death – all seemed to be hitting me at the same moment as I tried to see clearly enough to read the euthanasia consent form I was supposed to sign. This couldn't be happening, but it was.

I watched Dr. Harvey examine Ginny's poor, worn-out body. "Maybe I should have helped her die sooner. Most of her systems were shutting down," I said, hoping he didn't think I'd waited too long.

"There were reasons why you didn't do it until now," he responded.

In a last moment of ambivalence I wondered, "What if I don't help her die?"

"She would die from seizures if you don't help her die," he answered. That let me know I was doing the right thing. No more seizures for Ginny.

"It's the best thing, hardly any of them die easily by themselves. I just had to help some of my own die." he continued, filling the syringe with the liquid that would end Ginny's life.

Ginny whimpered when she felt the needle in her leg. Both Dr. Harvey and I clenched our teeth. I rubbed her back to comfort her. I didn't think she could hear me, but I said it just the same, "Just a minute and all the pain will go away." Those were the final words I said to her.

As the fluid traveled to her brain and heart, Ginny took one deep breath, and did not breathe again. I didn't need to ask Dr. Harvey to know that Ginny's life and spirit had left her body. She was dead. It was so fast. I wasn't sure I was even ready, and it was all over.

At first, my mind could not accept the reality of her death. She still felt so warm, and looked like she was just sleeping on her fuzzy pink blanket. Surely she would wake up in a few minutes and want to go home. It did not seem possible that she would grow cold; that I would have to bury her in the ground; that after 15 years Ginny would never again come bouncing out to greet me, or snuggle in my lap. The searing pain of loss stabbed my heart as Dr. Harvey reassured me that I had done the right thing.

After a time, Dr. Harvey started to wrap Ginny's body in her blanket. It didn't seem right to cover up her head, but he did. And that made her death start to feel more real.

Somehow I stumbled out of the hospital carrying the blanket with Ginny's still warm, limp body in it. Ginny's son, Pepi, who was waiting in the car for us, sniffed Ginny in her blanket and acted confused as we drove home through the cold April rain that matched our mood. But, even in my grief, I felt a sense of peace, of having done the right thing for Ginny.

At home Ginny's relatives sniffed her in her velvet-lined box, trying to use their sense of smell to figure out what had happened to her.

Her daughter Meg, the most intelligent of them all, gave me a puzzled and accusing look saying, "What did you do to her?"

"She was suffering too much, Meg. I had to," I tried to explain, hoping somehow she would understand.

Feeling very sad and emotionally shaken, I gathered Ginny's descendants around me for comfort, and did not try to work. That night we buried little Ginny's body wrapped in her pink blanket under a purple Rhododendron.

Even in the deep pain of loss during the following days, I felt such tremendous love, peace and joyful relief. The guilt I had anticipated was not there. Sometimes I wished I had chosen euthanasia sooner, but I knew I had not been emotionally ready to let go until the seizures. Comfort came from knowing I had done everything I wanted to for Ginny before her death. And, somehow, I just knew that Ginny's lively spirit was dancing around like a little sunbeam, delighted that finally I had released her from her dying body where she had been trapped until that April day.

CHAPTER 9

Mourning and Readjusting to Life

Mourning the Lost Relationship. Following Ginny's death, I had to work on a final letting go of my relationship with her. And you will have to do the same following the euthanasia of your pet. How much time this will take varies with each person. But, in general, if your pet died suddenly, you will have more letting-go work to do following the death than someone who had time to work on letting go before their pet died. Expect your letting-go work to be painful. Slowly, as time goes on, you will spend less time crying and mourning. You will be on the road to gradually recovering from your loss, assuming you have done the emotional work involved in each of the steps.

How will I feel after my pet's death? Grief is exhausting, so plan to get extra rest. You will feel lonely and need the support of friends or other animal lovers who will understand and tell you that you made the right decision. You will feel sadness, and need to take time to talk and write about your grief. Don't try to avoid or postpone your grieving. Express your feelings as they come up.

What actions can I take to help me readjust after my pet's death? Seek out the support of friends for reassurance during this time of mourning. Take time to feel your grief. The day your pet dies, don't try to work or put yourself into situations where you have to pretend you are feeling "okay." Don't expect to work at peak efficiency, concentrate, eat, or sleep very well for the next few days. Over time, the expression of your feelings will slowly decrease their intensity.

I'm afraid I will forget my pet. You will need to build a new relationship with your pet to keep his memory alive. Tangible objects such as photographs, or a favorite toy will remind you of your pet. Sharing stories about how he influenced your life, remembering you pet on special days, or making donations in your pet's memory are other ways to keep your pet "alive" for yourself. Many people continue to talk to their pets, or say they feel their pet's presence at times.

There is the question of whether and when to get another pet. The answer to this question will be different for every person. Most will need to grieve for awhile before making an emotional connection with a new animal friend. Chapter 19 discusses issues pertaining to bringing your next pet into your life.

Since adjusting to a changed life without your pet can be such an emotionally complicated process, I refer you to Chapters 19 and 20, *Tips for Adjusting to Life Without Your Pet,* and *A Final Meditation For The End Of Your Pet's Life,* where you will find many suggestions from other bereaved pet owners, and some final thoughts about the life and death of your pet, to help you through this most difficult time in your life.

Following the death of her horse, Sunny, Cheryl tried to follow the wisdom of injured animals. When animals are hurt, they withdraw from normal activities and go off by themselves while they heal. Cheryl didn't want to isolate herself completely, but she knew she needed to spend some time alone grieving. During her time alone, she read some of the books listed in the Bibliography, wrote about her feelings, and put together a photo album of her horse. She, also, participated in the Monday Evening Candle Ceremony on the Internet. Cheryl alternated her times alone with social times, during which she sharing her feelings and memories with understanding friends.

TAKE ACTION. What do you need to do to express your grief and help yourself adjust following your pet's death? How will you keep your pet's memory alive and pay tribute to his/her life?

CHAPTER 10

Families and Euthanasia

What about the pet who belongs to a family, and has multiple owners, each with his or her own individual grief reaction and needs at this difficult time? If you are thinking that multiple ownership makes for a complex reaction to pet euthanasia, you are correct.

A Family Faces Pet Euthanasia

When Dennis and Jeanne Winters received a diagnosis of terminal cancer on their 10-year-old Golden Retriever, Max, they decided to involve their four children in Max's death experience. The parents thought Max's death would help the children learn healthy coping behaviors at a time of loss. They recognized that each family member had a different type of emotional relationship with Max, and would miss Max in a different way.

For college student, Jamie, age 19, Max's death would sever a final link to his childhood.

Max's kisses and calm acceptance had helped Ben, age 15, through many teenage crises. Max slept in Ben's room at night, and Ben felt okay about hugging Max, although he felt awkward showing physical affection to family members.

The two younger children, Mickey, age 8, and Nichole, age 4, had no memory of not having Max as part of the family. Mickey played Barbie Dolls with Max, and fed him. Nichole loved to hug Max and have him kiss her. He liked to watch her make mud pies and would run races with her.

Max was wonderful company for Jeanne Winters when the children were at school. Dennis Winters liked to have Max sleeping by his chair at night while he read the newspaper.

TAKE ACTION. Describe the type of relationship and emotional involvement each member of your family has with your pet. What routines and rituals does each person have with your pet?

To cope successfully during this grief experience, the family members would need to support each other, permit different expressions and varying intensities of grief, and openly talk about the reality of approaching death and euthanasia. Everyone would have an opportunity to participate in the decision-making, and attend the euthanasia and funeral, if they wanted to do so.

Since the Winters children varied so widely in age, each child would have a different ability to understand death, and would require a different level of explanation and support.

Nichole, age 4, needed an explanation in clear, simple words she could understand. At this age, a child doesn't view death as permanent, and needs support more than detailed explanations. Her parents told Nichole that Max was very ill. His body was not working right, and was starting to die. The veterinarian was not able to help Max get better. When Max started to feel too much pain, they would all talk about helping Max die. Nichole's parents carefully avoided using the word "sleep" when describing death, so that Nichole would not equate sleep with death and become fearful of going to sleep.

Nichole's immediate reaction was to cry and scream, "No, No," when she heard this sad news. Children of this age loudly and openly express feelings instead of trying to cover them up as older children do. Nichole needed hugs from her parents, and she needed to hug Max. She had lots of questions. She was most concerned about whether the same thing that was happening to Max would happen to her.

Mickey, age 8, was old enough to understand more fully about death, and what was causing the illness. Between the ages of 5 and 9 children begin to view death as permanent, but think that it can be avoided, if they can figure out a way to do so. Mickey was trying to figure out a way to help Max avoid death as she asked to talk with the veterinarian.

Mickey's usual sunny disposition changed, and she became easily irritated. She had trouble falling asleep some nights, and experienced several nightmares. She hated to let Max out of her sight. When her parents encouraged Mickey to talk about what she was feeling and thinking, Mickey anxiously asked if parents ever got cancer and died. She wondered whether something she had done might have caused the cancer. Her parents reassured her she had not caused the cancer, and that, in the highly unlikely case they both got terminal cancer, they would have time to plan what relative would raise the children.

Their parents told Nichole and Mickey they could choose whether they wanted to be with Max when he died. The family would have to decide where to bury Max's body. The children could help make this decision, and help plan Max's funeral.

A new book about pet euthanasia, *A Special Place For Charlee - A Child's Companion to Pet Loss*, by Debby Morehead, comforted Mickey and Nichole. If your library does not yet have this book, you can order it from: Partners in Publishing, LLC., 5023 W. 120th Avenue, Suite 269, Broomfield, CO. 80020, Phone 303-438-5894 for $6.95 + shipping and handling. Their librarian also gave them a book called *The Tenth Best Thing About Barney* by Judith Viorst.

TO THINK ABOUT. Young children in a family need a clear explanation of death that will not create problems later on for them. Parents should NOT try to minimize, sugar-coat, or lie to children about a pet's death or euthanasia.

Unhealthy Explanations of Death	How Child Interprets
"Max has gone away on a trip."	Unclear. That means Max will probably return.
"God took Max because he wanted him in heaven."	Causes fear. What if God decides he wants me?
"Max died because he was sick."	Will I die, if I get sick?
"Death is an eternal sleep."	Will I die during sleep ?
"Max is now in heaven."	Unclear. Where/what is heaven?

Healthy Explanations of Death

"When Max died, his body stopped working. He can't breathe, eat, hear, see, go to the bathroom, or play with his friends anymore." This is a clear, factual explanation of death. It gives the child the message that it is okay to talk about this event called death. It answers a child's questions about the physical part of death.

"Max has died, and will never be alive again. We will miss Max. Right now we are feeling very sad. It will take time, but after awhile, we will remember Max without feeling quite so sad. We will always love Max and remember how wonderful he was, and all the fun we had with him." This is a complete explanation that encourages a child to talk about his feelings about death and loss. It acknowledges the pain, and offers hope of eventually moving beyond the hurt. If you don't acknowledge your sadness at the death of a pet, the child will get the idea that if he/she died, you would not feel sad either.

Ben, age 15, and Jamie, age 19, were old enough to hear and understand all the details available on Max's cancer and approaching death. They both understood that death was final and inevitable.

Ben was going to lose the one family member to whom he could express his feelings. The future looked pretty dismal without Max. Who would he walk and talk with? Who would listen and give him a kiss when everyone seemed to turn against him?

Ben felt angry and abandoned. He looked around for someone to blame. Maybe the veterinarian was to blame for not finding the cancer sooner. Maybe he himself was to blame. If he had noticed that Max wasn't feeling well, they could have found the cancer before it was impossible to save Max. Why did this happen to Max? Why couldn't it happen to the dog down the street who was chained outside and had bitten the mailman? His stomach and his head hurt so much. He was too old to cry the way his sisters did.

Ben was feeling all the common grief reactions teenagers and adults feel when confronted with terminal illness and death: the feeling of anger and looking for someone to blame, the questions about why Max instead of some other less-loved dog, the recognition of the important part Max played in his emotional life in these awkward teenage years, the embarrassment at crying at the death of a pet.

Ben's parents encouraged him to talk and write about his feelings. They stressed how important it was for him to have a voice in the family planning regarding euthanasia for Max, and later funeral and burial arrangements

When Jamie, age 19, looked at Max, he always remembered the good times the two of them had when he was a kid. He kept busy at school so he wouldn't feel sad and cry. But, when he came home and saw Max, it was hard to keep from crying. He tried to joke around to cheer people up, but the rest of the family just got angry.

The librarian recommended two books about pet death for older children: *The Yearling* by Marjorie Rawlings, and *Old Yeller* by Fred Gipson.

TAKE ACTION. *Based on your children's ages, decide how you would tell each of your children about the illness and upcoming euthanasia of a family pet.*

Guidelines To Help Children Get Through The Euthanasia Death Of a Pet:

♦ **Be honest with children.** Many parents try to overprotect their children from grief. Tell your children if their pet is going to die or need euthanasia. If you tell them a pet ran away, when you know it died or was euthanized, they will feel guilty and blame themselves because it ran away. Children have active imaginations, and will also worry about what terrible things might be happening to their runaway pet. If they ever find out you lied to them, they will no longer trust you.

♦ **Talk and cry with your children.** A child needs to express and share his grief, and you need to respect and encourage his need to do so. Never criticize a child for crying about the death of a pet.

Bring up the subject of the pet's death to show you are willing to talk about the subject. Don't assume you know how a child is feeling about the death of his pet — ask him. Encourage a child to talk by asking your child about his thoughts and feelings on death. The most helpful thing you can do is listen to your child's answers. Too many parents think they have to do all the talking. Just keep listening.

Don't tell your child to be strong, or praise your child for how well he is handling his grief. Statements like,"You are handling this so well," will keep a child from sharing his sadness with you.

When you are upset and need to cry and talk about your pet, don't run away from your children. If your children don't see you upset and crying, they will think their own sad feelings are wrong, and will not express them. They, also, might start to think that if they died, you would not miss them and feel sad. Children know when they are being excluded, and will learn to exclude you from their feelings, if you exclude them from yours. When your child grieves, ask what you can do to help.

♦ **Family members must respect each others feelings.** Some members in a family will grieve more deeply than others. This is a good time to teach children that, even though they don't feel as sad as someone else, they still must respect the other person's right to his feelings. *There is no such thing as right or wrong when it comes to the amount of grief someone feels.*

♦ **Don't get a new pet to "replace" the pet the child is grieving.** This will give the message that the relationship with the former pet was not important, and that the pet is easily replaceable. It makes light of the child's grief, and can anger the child.

♦ **Don't make unnecessary changes** in a child's life while he is grieving. This is not the best time to move to a new home or rearrange the furniture. Routines and stability are comforting.

♦ **Each family member is entitled to have a say in making an euthanasia decision about a pet's death.** Never euthanize a pet without telling the child, and helping the child understand why this decision has to be made. Try to get the child's permission for euthanasia. Allow plenty of time for the child to say goodbye to the pet before death. Include older children who are away from home in the decision-making process.

♦ **Individual family members have a right to decide exactly how much each wants to be involved in their pet's euthanasia.** Each child has a right to be present at their pet's death if they choose. Prepare them ahead of time for what to expect. It will be less traumatic for a child to witness a pet's peaceful death by euthanasia than to concoct some terrible fantasy of what it might have been like.

Preparing Children For a Pet's Euthanasia

Careful preparation of a child for pet euthanasia is one of the most important ways you can help a child start to deal with his feelings about death and euthanasia. The Winters family prepared their children for Max's eventual euthanasia in the following ways:

Family Discussion. The family gathered around the kitchen table one night and talked about Dr. Robinson's diagnosis and prognosis for Max. Included in this discussion was the cost of chemotherapy, the probable effectiveness of this type of treatment, and the quality of life they wanted Max to have. The children all agreed that they did not want Max to suffer.

Ben and Mickey had many questions about what euthanasia would be like for Max. How would it be done? Would it hurt? How long would it take? Could they be there, if they wanted to be? (They weren't sure they wanted to be there. It would depend on what was going to happen.)

Dennis Winters said he would schedule a talk for family members with Dr. Robinson. The appointment was set for 7 p.m. on Thursday.

Visit To The Veterinarian To Learn About Euthanasia
On Thursday night, Dennis and Jeanne Winters and a very apprehensive Ben, Mickey, and Nichole met with Dr. Robinson in one of the regular examining rooms where Max had received his checkups and shots since he was a 8-week-old puppy.

Dr. Robinson showed them a pink liquid in a bottle which he would put into a syringe, just as he would a regular shot. However, a regular shot helps an animal stay healthy, while this pink liquid helps an animal die, so it will not suffer any longer. Dr. Robinson stressed that pets are very lucky that euthanasia is available to end their suffering.

Max would lie down on the examining table, and Dr. Robinson would shave some hair from his front leg. Then Dr. Robinson would inject the pink liquid into a vein in Max's front leg. The pink liquid would first make Max fall asleep. When Max was asleep, the liquid would stop his heart from beating, and Max would die without feeling any pain. Mickey asked how long it would take. The answer was that it would be just a few seconds from the time Dr. Robinson injected the liquid until Max died. Nichole wondered if people get shots like this to die. Dr. Robinson explained that this is a wonderful, pain-free type of death that is only available for animals, not for people. Ben asked if they could be with Max when he died, and Dr. Robinson answered that anyone who wanted to be present could be there.

Asking Children If They Want To Be Present at Euthanasia
Their parents talked to Ben, Mickey, and Nichole individually to see whether they wanted to be present at Max's death. During this individual conversation with each child, the parents expressed their grief, and encouraged each child to express his/her grief. Each child was told to think about how he/she wanted to say goodbye to Max before he died. Jamie's parents phoned him at college to ask whether he wanted to be present when Max died.

The Euthanasia. A few weeks later, Max was feeling very ill. The Winters family sadly decided to phone Dr. Robinson to schedule an appointment on Saturday to help Max die. Each child spent time alone with Max to say a tearful goodbye. Nichole fluffed his ears one last time, Mickey tied a pretty scarf around his neck, and Ben and Jamie each spent some time alone with Max. Everyone fed Max favorite treats off their plates during the last meal before he died.

Max seemed to sense what was happening on Saturday as he picked up the grief and stress the family was feeling. Even though he felt very ill and wanted to die, he said a special goodbye to each child with a kiss and a slight wag of his lovely golden tail. The trip to Dr. Robinson's was very sad. They had to sign a permission paper when they arrived. Then they went into the examining room with Max. The entire family gathered around the examining table and watched as Dr. Robinson shaved the hair from Max's front leg, and filled a syringe with pink liquid which he injected into Max's leg. The family cried and hugged each other and Max. With a deep sigh, Max lost consciousness, and died peacefully almost as soon as the injection was given, just as Dr. Robinson had promised. Dr. Robinson listened to Max's heart, and told them Max "was gone." For a few minutes, everyone petted Max and cried. Mrs. Winters cut a piece of his golden fur to keep to remember him.

During Max's illness, the family had discussed the option of burial or cremation of Max's body. Later that day, they went to the cemetery where Max's body was put into a special dog casket they had purchased. The casket was taken to the grave where a granite marker with Max's name was already placed.

Each child had written something about Max's life, and read it as part of the funeral service for their good friend, Max. Dennis read some verses from the Bible. Mickey put Max's collar in the casket with him. Jeanne put in some flowers. Nichole put in his favorite ball he used to chase for her. Ben put in a letter no one else had seen. In the letter Ben thanked Max for all the times he had listened to him and loved him. Each person said a last tearful goodbye to Max before the casket was closed for the final time. As they left the cemetery, all the children promised Max they would never forget him, and would visit his grave often.

Continued Expression Of Grief Following Death. During the weeks following Max's death, Jeanne and Dennis continued to help the children express their feelings about Max's death. They knew that the death of such an important family member should not be minimized. They included the children in the following activities that would help them express their grief:

Activities to Help Express Grief

♦ **Draw pictures of your pet.** Mickey and Nichole drew pictures of Max wearing a halo and with two wings titled "Max in Heaven." They took them to *Show and Tell* in school the next day.

♦ **Compile a photo album of favorite pictures of your pet.** The children and parents shared many happy memories and tears as they looked through family photos taken over the past 10 years to choose special photos for " Max's Memory Book."

♦ **View home movies that include pictures of the deceased pet.** When family members felt ready, it was comforting to see movies of Max going about his daily life activities with the family.

♦ **Write and share memories.** Each child wrote a letter to Max, and shared it with the rest of the family. Some parts of the letters were sad, but some parts recalled happy times.

♦ **Play the "I Remember" game.** The Winters found it helped resolve guilty feelings, if they played the "I Remember" game and each shared what they remembered doing to help care for Max. Other times, when no one felt guilty, they played the "I Remember" game to share laughter and tears as they reminisced about their favorite memories of Max.

♦ **Read books about pet loss.** The librarian helped them find books about pet loss. The parents read the books to the younger children, and encouraged the older children to read and discuss the books with the rest of the family. (See the Bibliography)

Prolonged Grief Reaction. Both Jeanne and the teacher at school watched the children during the next several months for signs of a prolonged grief reaction. Fortunately, the children had enough support so they didn't experience the following symptoms of prolonged grief:

♦ Withdrawing from others.
♦ Clinging to parents or teacher. Refusal to go to school.
   Acting younger than their age.
♦ Frequent bad dreams or nightmares, seems tired all the time.
♦ Unusual irritability, moodiness or nervousness.
♦ Lack of interest in school or activities they once enjoyed
♦ Unwillingness to talk to you about their feelings
♦ Uncaring about how they dress or look.

Certainly, any of the above symptoms could have various causes. But if more than one of them had occurred suddenly, and continued within the month or two after Max's death, they could have been a sign of prolonged grief. If that had happened, Jeanne would have consulted a professional child counselor.

Bryan, A Child With Special Needs

The Winters family was a supportive, well-functioning family with two parents who had good communication with their children. They also knew about Max's illness, and had time to prepare themselves for the euthanasia. All families are not so fortunate.

Bryan, age 6, lived with his divorced mother and younger sister, Maria, age 4. Bryan's father lived in another state, and constantly broke his promises to visit his children. Bryan had been in play therapy for the past year because he was unable to directly express his sadness and rage about how his father was rejecting him.

Bryan repeatedly asked for a pet kitten, and his mother surprised him with one for his 7th birthday. Bryan immediately formed a very close bond with his new yellow kitten, Benji. Things went along fine for a few months, until one day Benji got out of the house and tried to follow his owner down the street. Benji was no match for the car that hit him that day. He was brain injured, and, several days later, Bryan and his mother chose an emergency euthanasia for Benji.

Everything had happened so fast, and Bryan was unable to express his grief and anger about the death of his friend, Benji. When Bryan came into therapy that next week, we read Mr. Rogers book, *When A Pet Dies*. Bryan sat expressionless through page after page of the story. Finally, near the end of the book, he burst into tears and asked for paper to draw a picture. Rapidly, he drew Benji with a mouth full of huge, sharp teeth opened in a snarl, and a cartoon over his head that said, "I am angry." He explained that Benji was angry because he had been run over by a car. From that day on, Bryan started to express his previously unexpressed anger and sadness about what his father was doing to him.

Drawing that one picture of his feelings seemed to help Bryan avoid having a prolonged grief reaction over Benji. In a few months, he was able to say he was ready for a new kitten. He soon formed a healthy bond with his new black kitten, Shadow, who stayed in the house and grew into a happy adult cat.

Existing Family Problems Complicate Pet Euthanasia

Throughout her life, Rosemary, age 40, had gone to a great deal of trouble trying to please her overly-critical mother. Needless to say, she was seldom successful. When Rosemary's favorite horse, Jupiter, was very near death, Rosemary's mother gave a big birthday party at her home in another state for Rosemary's father's 65th birthday.

Rosemary checked with the veterinarian and learned there was a high probability that Jupiter would have to be euthanized that very weekend. Since she wanted to be there to comfort Jupiter, she sent her regrets to her mother saying she could not attend the birthday party.

Rosemary's mother's total lack of understanding, and accusations that Rosemary didn't love her, hurt Rosemary deeply. Nevertheless, for the first time, she put her own feelings ahead of her desire to please her mother, and stayed with her horse. Her mother continued to remind her of her "lack of love" for many months.

Family members who are unsympathetic to the human-animal bond can create deep emotional problems for a pet owner who may be torn between his need to please that relative, and need to be with his pet at the time of death. Whichever choice the pet owner makes, will leave him feeling confused and guilty.

Family members, who don't understand the pain a pet owner experiences in choosing euthanasia and losing the companionship of a loved pet, make the loss of that pet all the harder to bear. Comments like, "You don't care as much about me as you did about that pet," can cut very deeply when one is grieving. If you feel confused or unable to get beyond the pain of such a cruel remark, try to get support from friends who will validate your right to feel your grief and meet your needs instead of doing what others want.

TO THINK ABOUT. You have a right to feel your grief over the death of a pet. You have the right to meet your own needs before you meet other people's needs.

Styles of Grieving

We each have our own individual style of grieving. Some people cry easily, and frequently, to release their sadness. Others are stoic, and cry very little, or at not all. A common stereotype in our culture is that men will "be strong," control their feelings, not cry, and not need any support at times of loss. The stereotype of women is that they will talk, cry, and need help from others while they grieve. These different styles of grieving may result in hurt feelings, family arguments, and even different opinions regarding medical treatment and euthanasia.

Frequent Crying Spells. Bill and Judy were going through the experience of choosing death for their German Shepherd, Lancelot. Bill was stoic, and did not show his grief with tears. During Judy's frequent crying spells, Bill felt uncomfortable and downright helpless. He tried unsuccessfully to stop Judy's tears by trying to cheer her up. Sometimes he teased her about crying so much. Sometimes he tried to problem-solve and find a way to make her feel happier. His suggestion that she just forget about Lancelot and keep busy the way he did made her cry even more. He became frustrated and angry when, despite his best efforts, Judy continued to cry. He told himself he also felt very sad, but he didn't go around crying all the time. Why did Judy? He just didn't understand.

Judy agreed that Bill did not understand her tears, or he would not keep trying to cheer her up. She angrily thought he acted like he didn't even care. She labeled his teasing as "cruel" and "insensitive."

Since Bill felt so helpless when Judy cried, Judy needed to tell Bill what he could do that would help her when she cried. She told him, "I feel better when I cry. When you see me crying, I want you to put your arms around me and hug me, but don't try to stop my tears." When Bill had some action to take, it helped take away his helpless feeling. Judy felt that Bill finally understood when he did what she had asked.

Irritability. When Bill felt the most sad, instead of crying, he became easily irritated. This was Bill's style of grieving, but Judy didn't understand this. She took his irritable moods personally, and wondered what she had done to cause his anger. When Bill realized that his irritable moods were the way he expressed his grief, he told Judy that instead of crying, he felt irritable when he was grieving. She had not done anything to trigger his anger. He also warned her in advance when he felt sad and irritable so she could stay away from him when he felt that way.

The challenge, in a household of family members who are grieving, is to identify each person's style of grieving and to be accepting of that person's individual grief expression. Some people like to be left alone while they are grieving. Some like to talk, cry, and share their grief with others. People don't always behave the way the stereotype suggests. Some men cry easily, and some women don't. All family members need space to express their grief in whatever way feels helpful for them. *There is no right or wrong way to grieve. Everyone grieves in their own way.*

TO THINK ABOUT. When dealing with grief reactions within a family, respect each others needs. Try to be supportive and understanding. Be willing to talk, listen, and cry with each other as the need arises.

CHAPTER 11

Emergency Euthanasia Guidelines

Your dog darts into the path of an oncoming car; your horse breaks a leg; your veterinarian finds untreatable cancer during exploratory surgery on your cat. Each situation involves untreatable or financially unaffordable illness or injury which will lead you to consider an emergency euthanasia decision. How do you go about making the decision?

Feelings As You Face An Emergency Euthanasia Decision. You will feel numb, overwhelmed, a sense of unreality, uncertain about what to do, confused, unable to think clearly, guilty and regretful that you haven't done something differently to avoid this situation. You may feel fear, panic, grief, frustration and/or anger.

You may say, "This can't be happening. It must be a bad dream. What do I do now? I can't even think. If only I had done . . . "

Preparing to Make the Decision. The shocked state of mind you are in at the time of a pet's sudden accident or illness is not helpful in making an irreversible euthanasia decision. Your first step, in such a crisis situation, is to *obtain information about your pet's medical condition* on which to base your decision.

Obtain Information to Make the Decision. Ask your veterinarian to examine your pet and answer the following questions about your pet's diagnosis, prognosis, and your available options:

Questions About Diagnosis, Prognosis and Treatment:
❖ *What is my pet's diagnosis and prognosis?*
❖ *What are my options?*
❖ *Is there any available treatment?*
❖ *If so, what is the percentage rate of cure with this treatment?*
❖ *How much pain would my pet suffer during treatment?*
❖ *Is there a chance my pet would die from the treatment?*

❖ *What is the cost?*
❖ *What kind of special home care would my pet need after treatment?*
❖ *Ask Yourself:*   *Can I afford the cost of treatment?*
❖ *Ask Yourself:*   *Could I provide special home care after treatment?*
❖ *Ask Yourself:*   *If I have time, do I want to get a second opinion?*

Following the veterinarian's diagnosis, prognosis, and recommendation, you may realize you are facing an euthanasia decision. *You will have to make the decision. The veterinarian should not make this decision for you.* Ask your veterinarian and yourself the following questions regarding your pet's quality of life:

Questions Evaluating Your Pet's Quality of Life:
❖ *Is my pet in constant or extreme pain?*
❖ *Is my pet able to move by himself?*
❖ *Can my pet eat and drink by himself?*
❖ *Can my pet walk?*
❖ *Can my pet interact with me and enjoy his surroundings?*

Decide Your Priorities and Make the Decision. Decide what your priorities are for yourself and your pet. If your pet is suffering, and your priority is that your pet not suffer, you may decide that choosing euthanasia would be the most loving gift you could give your pet.

Feelings Before and After Decision-Making. You may feel in shock and numb throughout the experience, but you might also feel fear regarding death and euthanasia, stress, anger, and guilt *before* making the decision. *After* making the decision, you might feel relief at having made the decision, sadness and the pain of loss, and peace that you can end your pet's suffering.

Ask your veterinarian the following questions in preparation for euthanasia:

Questions About Euthanasia:
❖ *Can I be present during euthanasia?*
❖ *Exactly what will happen during the euthanasia procedure?*
❖ *What medications will the veterinarian use?*
❖ *What will my pet experience?*
❖ *Will my pet know what is going on?*
❖ *Will my pet be awake or asleep?*
❖ *Will my pet feel pain?*
❖ *How long will it take?*
❖ *How will my pet's body react to dying?*
❖ *How will my pet's body look after death?*
❖ *Can I allow my children to witness euthanasia, if they want to?*

Children and Euthanasia. If your children want to be present at the euthanasia, it is okay. Just make sure they know what to expect. Also, get your veterinarian's approval. It will be reassuring for children to see that their pet's death is quick and painless. If your children are not present at the euthanasia, do not try to hide the death from them.

Additional Decisions You Will Be Called On To Make:

◆ **How to say goodbye.** Saying goodbye to your pet will help you accept her death. If your pet is suffering, you may have a limited amount of time to say goodbye. Ask to be left alone with your pet for a few minutes, and explain to her that you have chosen euthanasia to end the suffering. Also, thank her for sharing your life and bringing you so much joy.

◆ **Do you want to be present during euthanasia?** Although you may be nervous about witnessing euthanasia, your presence can be very comforting to your pet. You can be there for your pet the way she has always been there for you. Also, you will be reassured that your favorite companion had a quick, peaceful death. Knowing your friend has died will give you a sense of finality and closure which will help you in moving through your grief.

♦ **If you aren't there at the time of death, do you want to see your pet's body after death?** I encourage pet owners to see their pet's body for the reasons stated above. It helps with the problem of denial that death took place. If you haven't said goodbye, you could do so at that time. You might want to get a lock of hair.

♦ **Final arrangements for your pet's body after death.** You will have to decide whether to bury or cremate your pet's body. Refer to Chapter 18 for a complete discussion of your options.

Your Feelings After Your Pet's Emergency Euthanasia. Because you had no advance notice of death, you had little opportunity to express your grief before your pet died. You may have been in shock and felt numb through most of the experience. However, after death, those feelings will start to hit you with great intensity. Guilt, sadness, depression, anger, and loneliness are some of the feelings you can expect as you mourn.

Express your feelings in whatever ways feel right for you: through talking, crying, writing, art, music, or exercise. Don't try to avoid your grief feelings. Until you mourn, let go of your relationship with your living pet, and accept your part in your pet's death without guilt, your feelings will always be inside you ready to pop out at awkward moments. Releasing your grief may be complicated because it is more difficult to grieve without the physical presence of your pet, and our society is not supportive of mourning after a death. You may get the message, "out of sight, out of mind."

Places you can find supportive people include: a pet loss support group, or animal lovers on the Internet. These people will understand and encourage you to express your grief for as long as you need to do so. Spend lots of time writing and talking about your feelings. Expect the process to take time. Refer to Chapter 16, 17, and 19 for help in dealing with your feelings and adjusting to life after an emergency euthanasia.

CHAPTER 12

Euthanasia of a Healthy Pet

Earlier in the book we reviewed three myths that help us avoid thoughts that our pets will eventually grow old, become ill and die. There is a fourth myth connected with a dilemma that some pet owners find themselves in: the inability to keep a healthy pet.

Myth # 4: If I Can't Care For My Healthy Pet, I Can Find a Good Home For Her.

You are sure that if you put an ad in the paper, or put a sign on your veterinarian's bulletin board, you will find someone to adopt your pet. If you fail, the SPCA will find a good home.

Following his wife's death, Charlie's health failed, and he had to go into a nursing home. There was no way he could take his cat, Boots, into his new living arrangement. A notice on his veterinarian's bulletin board was lost among many other notices of pets who needed new homes. An ad placed in the newspaper did not produce any suitable home. Charlie's married daughter had a new baby, and was not able to take Boots. The woman at the SPCA said the chances were very slim that Boots would find a new owner. Most people wanted a kitten rather than a 10-year-old cat. Charlie found himself thinking seriously about choosing death for his friend, Boots.

The reality is that it is difficult, and often impossible, for you or the SPCA to find a good adoptive home for your pet. With the huge surplus of homeless animals, there is a high chance your pet will be euthanized at the SPCA. If you can no longer care for your pet, you may have to consider euthanasia for her.

The Steps of the Euthanasia Experience. Depending on how much time you have to find a home for your pet, this may be either a long-term or a crisis euthanasia experience. In either case, you will find yourself going through the steps of the euthanasia experience outlined in Chapter 2. If you have a crisis euthanasia, you will go through most of the steps after the death. If you have time, you will go through the steps prior to the death.

Doing Enough Before Choosing Euthanasia for a Physically Healthy Pet. As difficult as it is to make a decision to end the life of a dying pet, it is even more heartbreaking to choose death for a pet who is young or physically healthy. But sometimes life puts us in that dilemma. Problems like your own deteriorating health, the death of the pet's owner, a move to a home where a pet is not permitted, or a serious behavior or temperament problem are some of the circumstances that could lead to the euthanasia of a healthy pet. In cases like these, it is especially important that you feel you have done everything possible to find a new home, or to correct the behavior or temperament problem before choosing euthanasia. If you are unsuccessful in your attempts to resolve the problem, and must choose euthanasia, do not be too hard on yourself. Reassure yourself that you have done everything possible to save your pet. Explain the situation to your pet. Remind yourself that death will be quick and painless. Your pet will not suffer as he would if you turned him loose, and he starved to death, or was hit by a car.

Attempts to Find a New Owner. Asking friends, placing an ad in the local newspaper, or notifying your veterinarian are some ways to connect with a prospective adoptive home for your pet. Careful interviewing and screening of any applicants is crucial. There are unscrupulous persons who pretend to adopt a pet, only to sell it to labs for research.

Get a recommendation from their veterinarian, and visit the proposed adoptive home to get a feeling for how your pet reacts to the new person and environment. Plan several visits back and forth between the two homes to help with adjustment. Try to determine what the pet's life would be like with this person. Recognize how stressful a change of homes will be for your pet. It could take an adult pet months to adjust to a change in owners. Due to age or temperament, some pets just can't adjust to such a change.

Questions to Ask a Prospective Adoptive New Owner:
♦ *Why do you want this pet?*
♦ *Describe your family and your home and yard environment.*

♦ *Describe your daily routine, and how much time you would spend with the pet.*

♦ *What activities would you and the pet do together?*

♦ *Where would you keep this pet – night and day?*

♦ *Describe any other present pets.*

♦ *What other pets have you had in your lifetime? What happened to them?*

♦ *Obtain a reference letter from your veterinarian.*

♦ *Would you be willing to work out a series of visits between my home and your home so my pet can adjust slowly to the move?*

If you can't find a suitable home, or you know your pet would not be able to adjust to a new home, you will have to seriously consider euthanasia. But, you need to know you have done everything you could do before you decide to end your animal friend's life. Knowing you have done enough will help you deal with guilty feelings. And, just like the owner who has an ill or aged dying pet, you will need to complete all the other emotional work discussed throughout this book regarding the euthanasia of your pet.

I feel so guilty because I can't keep my pet. Keep in mind what efforts you have made to find a good adoptive home. Say goodbye to your pet, and apologize for your inability to continue to care for her. Explain that the other option of turning her loose would result in suffering for her. It's likely she would starve or be killed in some terrible way, since she isn't prepared to survive in the wild.

It will help to talk with someone who has been through the same experience, and has felt the same feelings. Talking with friends who have faced an euthanasia decision, members of a pet loss support group, a professional pet loss counselor, or understanding clergyman can reassure you that others have had similar feelings in connection with the euthanasia of a healthy pet.

Attempts to Correct a Temperament or Behavior Problem. With a serious temperament or behavior problem, such as problems with aggression, or failure to housebreak, you need to consult a professional who specializes in treating such problems. Some problems are resolvable, and some aren't. But at least you will know you tried to correct the problem before choosing euthanasia.

Questions to Ask a Pet Behaviorist:
◆ *How would you work to resolve this behavior problem?*
◆ *How much time would it take?*
◆ *How much would it cost?*
◆ *Do you guarantee results?*
◆ *Can I contact your references?*
◆ *What is your professional training and background?*
◆ *Can I be involved and watch you work?*
◆ *Ask Yourself: Does my pet feel comfortable with this person?*

As part of doing everything possible, Jim and Cary took their dog, Bret, to a pet behaviorist to try to modify Bret's increasingly aggressive attitude toward Jim. Jim had been bitten several times, and could not even approach his wife when Bret was near her. After multiple unsuccessful attempts to modify Bret's behavior, the behavior became even worse, and Jim was severely bitten in the face. At that point, Jim and Cary felt they had no option except to choose death for Bret. They felt extreme sadness, but comforted themselves with the knowledge they had tried every avenue they could think of before ending Bret 's life.

TO THINK ABOUT. **What do you need to do for your pet to feel you have done all you could to avoid euthanasia?**

Professionals Who Have Problems Euthanizing Healthy Pets. Some professionals find it quite upsetting to euthanize a healthy pet when they think a behavior problem could be corrected, or an adoptive home could be found. However, it does not mean the animal's life will be spared if you refuse to do the euthanasia. The pet's owner may find another, perhaps more painful, way to end his pet's life if you refuse euthanasia. You need to decide where you stand in regard to this dilemma, and why you feel the way you do. Once you decide, try not to go against your beliefs and values on a regular basis. As I mention in Chapter 6, to avoid excessive guilt about the euthanasia, you need to be able to justify to yourself why the euthanasia was necessary.

A Special Problem Connected With Obtaining Support.
You will find some people are judgmental and have angry reactions to the idea of euthanizing a healthy pet. Avoid such people as much as possible. Remind yourself of everything you did to find a good adoptive home, or to correct your pet's behavior or temperament problem. Remind yourself that, if you had turned your pet loose, he would have been frightened, and would have suffered a much more traumatic death than euthanasia.

The Importance of Self-Forgiveness. What do you need to do in order to be able to forgive yourself for any guilt you feel about choosing death for your pet? You need to:

1. **Know why you have to consider choosing death for your pet.**
2. **Acknowledge your feelings of guilt.**
3. **State exactly what you feel guilty about.**
4. **Compassionately understand your wish to avoid euthanasia.**
5. **Remind yourself of what you have done to try to resolve the problem and avoid euthanasia.**
6. **Know that it takes deep love and courage to make the euthanasia decision for your pet instead of walking away from the problem.**

TO THINK ABOUT. If you choose death for your pet with love in your heart, after doing everything you can do, you have saved your pet from a homeless future and further suffering.
YOU ARE INNOCENT.

PART II

DECISION-MAKING INFORMATION

CHAPTER 13

The Fine Art of Gathering Information

As you move through the steps of the euthanasia experience, you will face many decisions about your pet's life, medical treatment, and death. Making decisions and planning will give you a sense of strength and control as you face the death. The first step in making decisions and planning is to obtain information.

Who Will You Talk With To Gather Information?
♦ Your veterinarian can give you medical information.
♦ Friends who have been through similar illness can tell you what helped them, or what they would do differently.
♦ A pet behaviorist could work to overcome problem behavior.
♦ Prospective adoptive owners who might take a pet you can't keep.
♦ A professional counselor, if you feel too overwhelmed.

TAKE ACTION. Make a list of who you need to talk with to gather information.

What Types of Information Do You Need To Obtain? You probably have questions about your pet's diagnosis and prognosis, what your options are, available medical procedures, euthanasia, financial concerns, and how you can care for yourself as you go through this stressful experience.

Your Questioning Technique Is Important. You will have to ask the right questions in order to obtain enough information to make your decision. Short, direct questions are best. Each answer will logically lead to the next question, as in the lists of questions at the end of this chapter. Making up a list of questions you can work from will help you zero in on the important areas or points.

Listen to each answer before moving on to the next question on your list. The answer to the question you just asked may give you an opportunity to get even more information, if it leads you to another question that isn't on your list.

Try to clearly comprehend the answer. If you misinterpret what was said, you will be basing your thinking on faulty understanding. Therefore, don't be afraid to ask for clarification. "I don't understand what that means." or "Please explain further." are appropriate questions. You might repeat back to the speaker what you think you heard, just to check the accuracy of your understanding.

Most professionals will respect you for taking time to gather information prior to decision-making. If a professional doesn't have time for your questions, it is *his/her* problem, not yours. In such a case, you might consider finding someone else who has more time.

You may have a difficult time comprehending or remembering what your veterinarian says because you are stressed and grieving. Consider taking notes or tape recording your discussion. Take a friend along who can listen and help you recall what was said. You might need to schedule a follow-up session with additional questions at a later date. Don't be ashamed to do any of the above. Medical procedures and choosing death for your pet are all crucial decisions that are not reversible.

Getting a Second Opinion. Is it a good idea to get a second opinion by consulting another veterinarian? Sometimes your veterinarian will refer you to another veterinarian for specialized treatment of a complicated health problem. If your veterinarian doesn't refer you to another veterinarian, and you want a second opinion, that is your prerogative. Realize that a second opinion will cost you more time and money. But, if you want a second opinion to cover all bases, go ahead.

What will happen if you consult another veterinarian? The second veterinarian might agree with your veterinarian. Such a finding, would be reassuring because it would tell you that your veterinarian hasn't missed anything.

Or the second veterinarian could have an opposing viewpoint about your pet's condition and treatment. In such a case, you will hear both sides of the issue. If you are dealing with a health problem that has opposing viewpoints, it's a good idea to get as much information as possible so you can see both sides clearly before deciding what to do.

A warning. Before you search out another veterinarian, be sure you aren't just looking for one who will tell you what you want to hear.

Also, be sure you aren't looking for a veterinarian who will make the decision for you. You are the one who has to make any necessary decisions. It is your responsibility.

Sometimes people are afraid to ask questions because they are afraid of what the answers might be. Remember, *knowledge will help you feel in control.* One of the most frightening aspects of illness or approaching death is not knowing what to expect. Knowing *what* will happen, and *when* it might happen, will give you a better chance to be prepared and to feel in control – thus reducing your anxiety and fear.

The following questions will help you obtain the information you need: 1) to minimize the unexpected, 2) to understand what will happen each step along the way, and 3) to make decisions about what you want to do.

General Questions Regarding Communication With Your Veterinarian:

1. What hours can the veterinarian talk with me on the phone?
2. Can I reach my veterinarian anytime of the day or night?
3. Is there a different emergency phone number after hours?
4. Does my veterinarian carry a beeper? If so, what is that number?

Questions Regarding Your Pet's Condition:

1. **Ask Yourself:** Am I prepared to physically & emotionally deal with any negative, long-term side effects of treatment?
2. What is the diagnosis?
3. What causes the condition ?
4. Is there any available treatment?
5. Are there side effects of treatments? How long will they last?
6. How will the treatment help my pet? eliminate disability, pain?
7. Is there a chance my pet will die from the treatment?
8. Do I have to decide between various forms of treatment?
9. How long will my pet need the treatment ?
10. What is the percentage rate of cure with this treatment?
11. How much additional time will the treatment give my pet ?
12. Will the additional time be pain-free?
13. How long will my pet have to stay in the hospital?
14. What is the cost of any available treatments?

Questions Regarding Tests:
1. What is the purpose of these tests?
2. How painful are they?
3. What will be done to my pet during the tests?
4. What risks are involved?
5. When will I know the test results?
6. What would happen if the tests aren't done?
7. How much will the tests cost?
8. Will more tests need to be done later?

Questions Regarding Medications:
1. Will the medications cure my pet?
2. Will the drugs give my pet extra time? If so, how much?
3. What symptoms will the medications help?
4. What are the common side effects?
5. What will happen if my pet doesn't take the drugs?
6. How difficult are the drugs to administer? Can I do it?
7. How much will the drugs cost?

Questions Before Surgery:
1. What are the risks and benefits of this surgery?
2. Is there a chance my pet might die during surgery?
3. What are the alternatives to surgery, their benefits and risks?
4. Will my pet have pain after the surgery?
5. How much will surgery cost?
6. What are the risks of anesthesia?
7. What is my pet's prognosis, if I decide against surgery?
8. How soon can my pet come home after surgery?
9. What kind of special home care will my pet need after surgery?
10. How long will it take my pet to recover from surgery?

Questions About Costs:
1. How much is my bill now before any further procedures?
2. What will each separate procedure cost?
3. What would the total cost of all treatment be?
4. What would the cost be for euthanasia?
5. Can I pay in advance for the euthanasia?

6. Does the hospital have arrangements for a deferred payment plan?
7. **Ask Yourself:** How much are you able or willing to spend?

Questions About "Natural Death" vs. Euthanasia:
1. If I let my pet die a natural death, what will that death be like?
2. How much pain will my pet have?
3. Can the pain be controlled by medication?
4. What body systems will fail before death?
5. How will that affect my pet's body and behavior?
   (Will there be seizures, coma, gasping for breath, cries of pain?)
6. How much care will my pet need?
7. If I don't euthanize, approximately how long will my pet live?
8. **Ask Yourself:** Will I be able to care for my pet at home?

Questions About Euthanasia:
1. Can I be present during euthanasia?
2. Exactly what will happen during the euthanasia procedure?
3. What medication will the veterinarian use?
4. What will my pet experience?
5. Will my pet know what is going on?
6. Will my pet be awake or asleep at the time of euthanasia?
7. Will my pet feel pain?
8. How long will it take?
9. How will my pet react?
10. What will my pet's body do? (phantom deaths, urination).
11. Can I pay for the euthanasia in advance?

Questions About Your Resources:
1. How much of my time will caring for my ill pet take?
2. What other responsibilities do I have in my life?
3. Do I have a partner, children, job, other pets?
4. What effect will this care have on my marriage, children, job, friends, pets?
5. Do I have any family members or friends who can help?
6. What other stresses do I have in my life?
7. At what point will my emotional resources become exhausted?

8. Will my pet's illness interfere with vacations?
9. How much am I able or willing to spend on my pet's illness?

Questions About Your Veterinarian:
1. Do I want to see another veterinarian for a second opinion?
2. Do I feel I can talk to my veterinarian and get the answers to my questions?
3. Is my vet emotionally supportive? Would I feel okay crying in front of him/her?

Questions To Ask Friends:
1. What was it like when you went through a similar experience?
2. What did you or others do that was helpful?
3. What would you do differently another time?

Questions To Ask a Mental Health Professional:
1. What feelings can I expect as I make a euthanasia decision?
2. What feelings can I expect to have as I grieve?
3. Do I appear to be "stuck" in my decision-making?
4. Do I appear to be "stuck" in my grief?
5. What is the best way to work through any issues where I appear to be stuck? How long will it take?

TAKE ACTION. Decide which of the above questions you need to ask before making your decisions.

CHAPTER 14

Decision-Making Tips

In addition to the euthanasia decision, there are other decisions you will be called on to make when your pet is dying:

♦ Whether to choose medical testing and treatment: if so, how much?
♦ When to schedule the euthanasia?
♦ Whether you want to be present to comfort your pet at the time of death, if you choose euthanasia? (See Chapter 15 for reasons why it is helpful to be present).
♦ Where do you want your pet to die: at your home, or at the veterinarian's office?
♦ How do you want to say goodbye to your pet?
♦ Whether you want to see your pet's body, if you aren't there when it dies?
♦ What do you want done with your pet's body after death?
♦ If you choose burial, where will you bury your pet?
♦ If you choose cremation, who will do the cremation, and what do you want to do with the ashes?
♦ How do you want to pay tribute to your pet's life?

Making a good decision can give you a feeling of control and power in a situation where you initially feel helpless and out-of-control. Just as euthanasia is a journey into the unknown for most of us, so decision-making about matters concerning death may also be a journey into the unknown. Let's take time to review the six steps of effective decision-making.

A word of caution. Because of the complexity of the feelings and issues that must be dealt with prior to euthanasia, this decision-making model is too simplistic to use in making your euthanasia decision. Be sure you have gone through the steps outlined in the first part of this book, before you make a final pet euthanasia decision.

The decision-making process involves six steps. They will guide you as you use logic, feelings, your values, and take your personal circumstances into consideration in order to reach your decision. You will use the following steps:

---

1.   A. Define your problem situation
     B. State your priorities for yourself and your pet.
2.   Gather detailed factual information.
3.   List all your options.
4.   Observe whether each option triggers positive
     or negative feelings for you.
5.   State your preferences and rank them.
6.   Make the decision.

■   *Step One:* **A.** *Define Your Problem Situation.*
                 B. *State Your Priorities For Yourself
                 and Your Pet.*

A. The first step in decision making is to clearly define the problem situation. You might say, "I need to plan for the medical treatment of my dying pet."

TAKE ACTION. Try to clearly define your own problem situation.

B. Next, state your priorities. What do you want for yourself, and what do you want for your pet as the outcome of your decision-making?

If your pet is dying, you might state your priorities as: 1) Wanting your pet to live as long as possible. 2) Not wanting your pet to experience a lot of pain.

TAKE ACTION. What are your top priorities – for yourself and for your pet? Write down one or more priorities.

As a result of this first step, you may think you know exactly what you want. Or you may find that you are not yet completely certain of what you want. Either way, it's okay. As you go through the material in this exercise, you can continue to define what is it you want for yourself and your pet.

■   *Step Two:* *Gather Detailed Factual Information*

During the second step, you gather as much information as you need to make your decision about the problem.

Decide who you want to talk with to gather the information, and what questions to ask. Keep your stated priorities from Step 1 in mind while you gather information.

TAKE ACTION. Refer to Chapter 13 for possible questions to use while gathering information.

■   *Step Three:* *List All Your Options*

During the third step, you look at all the information you have collected, and list all your options. Don't rush through this process. Time will give you a chance to really think, and list as many options as possible. As you move through this third step, you may be relieved to realize that you do have a wide range of choices available to you.

This is *not* the stage where you make a decision. Allow yourself to be indecisive, and don't decide on any one option as you make your list.

TAKE ACTION. What are your options ? List all your options.

■   *Step Four:*   *Observe Whether Each Option Triggers Positive or Negative Feelings For You.*

At this step, let a free flow of feelings and thoughts come up to your consciousness about each of the various options you have identified. Let the feelings and thoughts come up at their own speed. Don't try to block them, and don't try to rush them either. Don't make any impulsive decision to take action. Just observe what thoughts and feelings come up whenever you think of each of your choices.

This is a very critical step in the decision-making process, and, yet, it is a stage that some people skip. During this stage you are using the left (logical side) of your brain to observe the thoughts that come from the left side of the brain, as well as the feelings that come from the right (feeling) side of your brain.

You may notice, over a period of time, that each choice seems to repeatedly trigger the same feelings. Some choices you will feel uneasy or troubled about, and some choices will seem fairly acceptable. What is happening is that your values and priorities are being linked in your mind with each of your choices to produce positive or negative feelings.

For example, if you are making decisions about medical care, and are short on funds, you will feel anxious when you think about expensive medical procedures. Or, if you don't want your pet to suffer, you might feel anxious if you know certain medical procedures would cause your pet needless pain without extending your pet's life for very long. If you want to provide all available medical care for your pet, and can afford it, you might feel pleased when you think about the availability of extensive medical care.

Trouble At Step 4. You could run into trouble at this stage if you don't recognize what your feelings are about your different options, or if you let others make your decisions. If you go against your own feelings and make this decision to please someone else, you will be setting yourself up for future guilt.

TO THINK ABOUT. It is important to take time to get in touch with your feelings in preparation for making your decisions.

■   ### Step Five: State Your Preferences and Rank Them

Here you will state your preferences (which come from your true feelings) and rank them from most to least desirable. What if two of your preferences are in conflict? For example, your desire that your pet not suffer might be in conflict with your wish that your pet live as long as possible. You must choose which has the highest priority.

TAKE ACTION. What are your preferences? State them, and list them from most to least desirable.

■   ### Step Six: Make The Decision

After ranking your priorities, you will move ahead to making your final decision – one that feels right for you and your pet.

Take Action. What is your final decision? Do you feel comfortable with your decision?

Decision-Making Points to Remember

♦   You do have options.

♦   No decision is ever perfect. There is some attraction about each option you have discarded.

♦   Take time to think before deciding what to do.

♦   If you feel unsure, take more time to think.

♦   Don't act or refrain from acting because you're afraid of what others will think.

♦   There is always something else you could have done. When have you done enough?

CHAPTER 15

What to Expect During Pet Euthanasia

Do you want to be present when your pet dies? There are three reasons why many pet owners decide they do want to stay with their pet during the death experience.

First, there is a tendency for your mind to deny that death has really taken place. "I don't believe it" or "It doesn't seem real" are common reactions to the news of a death. If you are not present at the death, or do not see the dead body, it is possible to remain in a state of disbelief indefinitely. In fact, a death from euthanasia is so rapid and peaceful that it is sometimes difficult to believe that your pet has actually died, even though you witnessed it. In the long run, it does help you to accept the death if you were there when it happened.

A second reason you might want to be present with your pet at death is to assure yourself that your favorite companion had a peaceful, easy death. If you were not present, your imagination might conjure up an upsetting death scene and stir up guilty feelings. If you were there, you know that nothing upsetting happened for your pet at the end of life.

Perhaps, the most important reason of all to stay with your pet while the injection is given, is to be there for your pet the way your pet has always been there for you. Many pets become nervous away from their owners, and your presence will be comforting.

Maybe, before you make your decision, you need to know the answer to the question: what will happen when your veterinarian helps your pet die? At one level, you probably don't want to think about what will happen. But, at another level, you need to know. This knowledge will make you more comfortable with your euthanasia decision. It will prepare you, if you decide to stay with your pet when it dies.

The following information is a general outline of common euthanasia procedures. Prior to the euthanasia of your pet, you should talk to the veterinarian about exactly how he will do the euthanasia.

The drug most commonly used for euthanasia is called Pentobarbital. It is a pink or blue Windex-type color. Your pet will feel no pain once the drug is administered because it affects both the brain and the heart. Pentobarbital contains an anesthetic that works on the brain to put the pet to sleep, and a second ingredient that stops the heart after the pet goes to sleep. The amount of Pentobarbital administered is determined by the weight of the animal. A small pet will receive several CCs from a syringe. A 1000 pound horse will need 120 ccs (two syringes full). Usually the drug works within seconds – a few seconds for a small pet, and up to 20-30 seconds for a horse.

A houschold pet usually receives the injection in a vein in the front leg. If the pet has long hair, the veterinarian will shave some of the hair from the front leg so he can find the veins before giving the injection. An alternative procedure is to put a catheter into the rear leg of the pet. The Pentobarbital is then injected into a tube which extends from the catheter. If the pet is extremely small, or an infant animal with tiny veins, the injection may be given directly into the heart. A horse receives the injection in the jugular vein in it's neck. If the horse's body is to be used for meat, the horse is shot in the head so that it loses consciousness instantly.

If you take your pet to the veterinarian, both the veterinarian and the veterinarian technician will probably be in the room with you. Ask whether you can hold your pet during the injection. Some veterinarians want a small pet to lie down on the examining table for the injection. In that case, you or the veterinary technician can hold your pet as soon as the injection has been given. A very large pet would lie on the floor, and you could hold your pet's head.

Large veterinary schools often have a home-like comfortable setting for pet euthanasia. They set aside a special room where a family and their pet can gather. The family will hold their pet on their lap and comfort it, and each other, at the time of the death.

Most pets become anxious when they go to the veterinarian's office. If you want your pet to die in familiar surroundings, ask your veterinarian if he will come to your home. Some veterinarians offer this service. If the veterinarian comes to your home for the euthanasia, you can choose your pet's favorite spot – indoors or outdoors – where you think your pet would be most comfortable. Some cats have a favorite sunny spot, or a dog might have a favorite bed, or a favorite tree he likes to sleep under out in the yard.

The thousand pound weight of horses makes the location of the euthanasia critical. A horse who is to be buried, will be euthanized next to the grave, so it will fall into the grave as it loses consciousness. If the entire body of the horse is not going to be buried, it will be euthanized in a padded stall or in a small, fenced-in area.

Every veterinarian and pet owner wants the pet's death to be a swift, easy transition from life to death. However, certain conditions may make the euthanasia more difficult, and potentially upsetting for the pet owner. It's important to understand where complications may arise, if you want to stay with your pet during euthanasia.

Your pet's state of mind will greatly affect how peacefully he dies. If your pet is extremely nervous, or aggressive and struggling, it will make the injection more difficult to give, and could be upsetting for you to watch. Your veterinarian will probably prepare you, if he anticipates this will be the case.

If a horse is feeling well enough, he is usually standing when the injection is given. Many horse owners find it upsetting to see their horse fall down as it loses consciousness, so may opt not to watch the euthanasia.

Additional complications arise if a pet is very old. Often the veins collapse, making injection of the Pentobarbital difficult. If the pet's heart is weakened by illness or old age, the circulation is slower, and the drug will travel more slowly through the pet's body, so death will come more slowly.

Most pets look as though they are sleeping after they die, except that their eyes are open. However, death is not pretty. Some sights and sounds associated with a dead body can be upsetting, if you are not prepared for them. The eyes and mouth are open after death. Usually the tongue protrudes from one side of the mouth. Sometimes air leaving the lungs after death can make a gurgling sound. Occasionally there are muscle tremors, which can continue a few minutes after death, and may even look like a mild seizure. The loss of body fluids, urine, and feces are very common after death. Following injury in accidents and some illnesses, blood may come from the ears, nose, mouth, and rectum. If you will be spending time with your pet's body as you transport it home for burial, you need to be prepared for these sights.

If you decide you don't want to be present at the time of your pet's euthanasia, talk to your veterinarian about who will be present to comfort your pet when the injection is given. Most veterinary hospitals have a technician who helps the veterinarian, and who will be there loving and comforting your pet as it dies. Kim, the technician who helped me with this part of the book, said she holds and comforts pets when the owner is too upset to be present at the euthanasia. It is a very sad time for veterinarians and their staff when they have to help a favorite pet die. Many of them cry along with the owner. I've heard of one veterinarian who tells the pet over and over as he gives the injection, "You are loved."

For five and a half long years Margaret and her friendly diabetic white poodle, Chrissy, made the trip to the veterinary hospital for Chrissy's daily injection of insulin which Margaret's arthritic fingers were unable to administer. Chrissy made many friends, and became a kind of a hospital mascot during her daily visits. Finally, one Valentine's Day, Chrissy's condition worsened, and Margaret knew she had to ask Chrissy's doctor to help her die.

That terrible Valentine's Day the hospital staff cried with Margaret over Chrissy's death. To express their sorrow, they decorated a box with Chrissy's name surrounded by valentine hearts and flowers in which Margaret could bury their favorite dog. Margaret said she will always remember how the hospital staff's love for Chrissy comforted her in her grief.

TAKE ACTION. Are there any questions you want to ask your veterinarian about the euthanasia procedure? Do you want to stay with your pet during the euthanasia?

PART III

SELF-CARE DURING
THE EUTHANASIA EXPERIENCE

CHAPTER 16

Surviving Your Feelings

Thinking about choosing death for your pet will stir up lots of upsetting feelings. You will feel more in control if you know in advance what those feelings will be, and how to express them.

Feelings create energy inside your body. It is healthier to express your feeling energy than to keep it stuffed down inside. As we discuss each feeling, I will suggest various ways to discharge the energy stirred up by that feeling. Not every technique I mention will be right for each person. Some people find direct physical release of feeling to be most helpful. Others find visualization or writing activities helpful. Experiment, and select whatever techniques feel right for you.

Guilt

Guilt Over Choosing Death For Your Pet. You can expect to feel guilty if you are thinking about choosing the hour of your pet's death. Guilt is a common reaction to death, even when you have no responsibility for the death. By asking someone to kill your pet, your guilt could be intensified. You will have a specific act to hang your guilt on when it surfaces.

If your pet is ill or aged, it may be helpful for you to remind yourself that you are *not* responsible for your pet's ultimate fate. The aging process, temperament problem, or disease that brings your pet to the end of it's life is out of your control. If you can no longer keep a loved pet because of a change in your personal circumstances, that is often out of your control.

TO THINK ABOUT. You are not responsible for the end of your pet's life. You are only the agent who will help your pet leave its worn-out body with less suffering than nature would decree.

Guilt Over Matters Other Than Euthanasia. In addition to feeling guilty over helping your pet die, you may also feel guilty about other things such as: not spending enough time with your pet, not appreciating your pet enough while it was alive, or losing your temper with your pet. With an ill pet, you may wonder whether the medical treatment made your pet worse. Maybe you should have used a different veterinarian. Did your pet's food or lifestyle cause this illness? In fact, if you look hard enough, you can usually find something else you could have done, or something you could have done differently.

You might feel vaguely guilty, and not even know why you feel guilty. It probably doesn't feel right that your pet is sick or dying, while you still are alive and healthy.

It's gotten to the point where, when I am grieving, I will say (preferably before I start feeling any guilt), "I wonder what I will feel guilty about in connection with *this* death?"

TO THINK ABOUT. If you prepare yourself ahead of time to expect to feel some amount of guilt, it helps to normalize the guilty feelings so they don't get blown out of proportion when you experience them.

Dealing With Your Guilt. The first step in dealing with your guilt is to acknowledge that you are feeling guilty.

Next, you might find it reassuring to give yourself factual messages about the reality of your pet's life and death, and your competency as a pet owner. Use the following list as a guide. Put your pet's name in wherever it says "My pet." You might even want to write down the answer to any questions that apply to you.

Things to Tell Yourself When You Feel Guilty.

1. "My pet (name) was at the end of his life. The reason I know this is . . . " (list symptoms of approaching death, pet's age, etc.)

2. "I chose euthanasia for my pet (name) because he was suffering. The ways he was suffering include: . . . "

3. "I took excellent care of my pet (name) while he was alive." List everything you did to care for your pet – include feeding,

grooming, exercise, medical care, playtime, attempts to overcome temperament or behavior problems, attempts to find a new home.

4. **"I took excellent care of my pet (name) as he approached death."** List anything you did to care for your pet at the end of his life: medication, medical tests or treatments, special feeding, or handling, etc. Remind yourself of the time, energy and money this took.

5. **"If I did not love my pet (name), I would not be so upset now."**

How You Kept Your Pet Alive. If your pet had a long illness, you might find it helpful to ask yourself if your pet, in his present condition, would still be alive if he were living in the wild. Is he strong enough to move around to escape predators? Does he still see and hear well enough to escape predators? Could he hunt food, and eat and drink by himself?

If the answers to any of these questions is "no," your pet is alive because of you. You have actually kept your pet alive beyond his normal life span. It's important to give yourself credit for what you have done up to this point in time to prolong your pet's life.

TAKE ACTION. Write down exactly what you have done to extend your pet's life since he became too ill to survive without your intervention. You can refer back to what you have written whenever you start feeling guilty.

It Was My Fault That My Pet Was Involved In An Accident That Led To The Euthanasia. If some guilt is justified because you were realistically at fault for an accident that led to your pet's euthanasia, it will help you to talk about your guilty feelings. It will also help to take some action. I often suggest writing down what you would like to say to your pet, perhaps some kind of goodbye statement, or even an apology. You need to forgive yourself. Remember that pets are very forgiving, and would not be as hard on you as you are on yourself. If this terrible experience has taught you a positive lesson about some danger to animals, maybe you can warn others by writing something that other pet owners can read.

Talking With Your Pet About Dying. Are you feeling guilty because your animal friend is not able to communicate verbally to you what his wishes are about his life and death? Pets don't make living wills we can refer to when they are close to death.

Try talking to your pet about your guilty feelings. Most people talk to their pets from time to time, so please don't feel silly about the idea of talking to your pet about this most important decision.

Even though your pet can't tell you verbally what he wants, there is much nonverbal communication that takes places between the two of you. You talk, and your pet responds with looks and actions – a kiss or a touch.

Let's review the discussion in Chapter 7 of how to talk with your pet about euthanasia: Look into your pet's eyes to get his attention, and tell him how you feel about what he is going through. Explain what you are feeling about losing him. Talk to him about all you have done to avoid euthanasia as long as possible. Explain that modern medicine can prolong his life, and possibly his suffering, for a very long time. Ask your pet how he feels about your making arrangements to end his suffering and release him from his ill or infirm body. Tell him that you want to make the best decision for him – the decision he would make for himself, if he could. Ask your pet what he would like you to do.

You and your pet have probably always had a great deal of nonverbal communication. Use that nonverbal communication now with your pet. Be still, empty your mind, be receptive, and see if you can pick up any feelings from your pet about what he/she would like to have happen in this matter of life and death. What words come into your mind as you ask your pet this question, and listen for his answer?

Most pets are very intuitive, and, if they are not too ill, will respond in some way to what you are saying to them. Your pet's response can go a long way towards helping you feel comfortable with making a decision that is right for both of you.

How do you feel after talking this decision over with your pet? How do you think your pet feels about your talking with him regarding the option of euthanasia? How do you feel about what you think your pet has communicated to you?

If Your Pet is Deceased, you can write a letter to your pet, expressing your thoughts and feelings about your past decision to choose death for her. Picture your pet in your mind or look at a picture of her as you write. Imagine what she would do or say in response to your letter. You might even want to write a letter back to yourself from your pet expressing the feelings you think she would want to communicate to you.

The release of feelings as you talk or write can be very healing, and will help you deal better with your guilt.

TAKE ACTION. **Talk to your pet about euthanasia and your guilty feelings. If your pet is no longer alive, write a letter to your pet about your feelings.**

Guilt About Medical Issues. It helps with grief if you understand the medical facts surrounding the final illness or death. If you have unanswered medical questions after your pet's death, schedule an appointment to talk with your veterinarian to obtain the information. Sometimes, additional medical information about the cause of death can help with lingering guilty feelings about what you might have done differently.

Reliving The Past To Stay Connected. If your pet has already died, it is important not to stay trapped in guilt by constantly reliving the past. Remind yourself that you can't go back into the past and change any behaviors you regret. If there are actions you regret, resolve to learn from them, forgive yourself, and go on from here.

Some pet owners constantly relive their pet's final moments and their feelings of guilt about the death *as a way of staying connected* with their pet. They fear, if they let go of their pet's death, they will somehow forget their pet.

Bob chose death for his dog, Jake, after Jake was hit by a car which left him alive, but with extensive brain damage. Bob kept seeing Jake running in front of the car. Every time Bob replayed this scene in his mind, it kept Jake alive for Bob. It also brought up major guilty feelings that Bob had not kept Jake on his leash that fateful day. I suggested that Bob try playing some earlier happy scenes of Jake in his mind – scenes that would not leave him feeling so guilty, but which would help him continue to feel connected to Jake.

Give yourself permission to move beyond your guilt. Substitute memories of happy times during your pet's life for the final death and illness scenes you keep playing over and over in your mind. You will not forget your pet, if you substitute happy memories for sad memories.

TO THINK ABOUT. *You can stay connected to your pet by remembering happy scenes of your pet's life.*

The Importance of Self-Forgiveness. What do you need to do in order to be able to forgive yourself for any guilt you feel about choosing death for your pet? You need to:

1. *Identity the reason you have to consider choosing death for your pet.*

2. *Accept the fact that it is your responsibility to make this decision.*

3. *Acknowledge your feelings of guilt.*

4. *Identify exactly what you feel guilty about.*

5. *Compassionately listen to your desire to avoid this painful decision.*

6. *Love yourself, and know that you are innocent of any wrong-doing .*

7. *Know that it takes tremendous love to consider taking an action that will release your pet from his suffering, while it leaves you with so much pain.*

TO THINK ABOUT. What do you need to do in order to forgive yourself for feeling guilty about choosing death for your pet?

Relief

If your pet has been ill, you will feel great relief when your pet's suffering ends through death, or when you make the euthanasia decision to end your pet's suffering. You feel relief because:

1) the decision is finally made
2) your pet will no longer be in pain
3) you are ending the stress of caring for your ailing pet

Remember the medications that your pet didn't want to take, the times you had to clean up after him, or carry him around, or hand feed him when he didn't want to eat. All this time-consuming inconvenience is now ended.

What if you feel guilty for feeling so much relief? You might even wonder if you killed your pet for your own convenience? Believe me, feeling relief is a normal reaction after a loved one's stressful dying experience. If you talk with others who have been through a similar illness and death, you will learn that relief following the death of a loved one is common. Remind yourself of all you did to lovingly care for your pet during his dying time.

TO THINK ABOUT. You did enough. It was time to let go.

Fear

Fear is a powerful, negative emotion that has the power to paralyze you so you can't get beyond it. To effectively deal with any fear you need to:

1) Acknowledge the fear.
2) Try to clearly understand what it is you are afraid of.
3) Assess how valid the fear is.
4) Decide what action to take to overcome the fear.

Fears Connected With Euthanasia Include:

Fear of Death.

"I've never had anyone this close to me die."
"What will it be like for my pet?"
"What will it be like for me?"
"Is there some sort of life after death for pets?"

Facing death can be terrifying. This is especially true if you have never gone through the death experience with someone you love. In a way, you are dealing with feelings about your own death, as you share your pet's death experience. So your pet will be your teacher as you learn about death. Consult your veterinarian, friends, your clergyman, or a professional grief counselor for ideas about what to expect during your pet's dying time.

Fear of Killing.

" I've been taught that killing is wrong".
"How can I plan the death of someone I love?"
"It feels like murder."

Our society does not find a planned death for human loved ones acceptable. Now you are told that it is okay to end your pet's suffering with euthanasia. It can be psychologically overwhelming for your mind to deal with this contradiction in values. So, is it any wonder you feel terrible distress? Chapter 6 discusses euthanasia as a loving and positive use of power to end suffering. It may help in your thinking about this issue.

Fear of the Euthanasia Procedure.

"Exactly what will happen during the procedure?"
"Will my pet know what is going on?"
"Will my pet feel pain?"
"What will I experience?"

Euthanasia is a spooky, mysterious, scary experience. We don't even want to think about what happens during the euthanasia procedure, and yet we need to know in order to reduce our fears. All those questions that are so difficult to ask need to be discussed with your veterinarian. Chapter 14 will also help answer your questions about euthanasia.

Fear of Dealing with Conflicting Roles.

"How can I be a loving owner, if I'm thinking about putting my pet to death?"
"How can I live with myself, if I plan my pet's death?

Even thinking about euthanasia puts you in the opposing roles of loving pet owner and executioner of your loved one. How can your mind reconcile these conflicting roles? The answer to these questions is love – the kind of love that puts someone else's suffering before your own. But it will take you time to struggle with and resolve these questions before you can have peace over choosing death for your pet.

This book will help you identify and validate your feelings about these opposing roles. Talking and writing about your feelings will also help you deal with this fear.

Fear of Feelings.
"What feeling will I have if I choose euthanasia?"
"How can I deal with my feelings – especially guilt?"

Because human euthanasia is not legal, there are no parallels in human experience for what you can expect to feel if you choose death for your pet. Expressing whatever feelings you have is the most helpful thing you can do for yourself. Don't try to stuff feelings down inside. Don't feel silly for acknowledging the feelings you have. Find people you can talk with who will validate your feelings because they have gone through a similar experience.

Fear of Crying in Front of Others.
"Will people think I'm nuts for being so upset over a pet's death?"
"Will they think less of me because I cried?"
"What if I can't stop crying?"

Expressing your sadness by crying is a healthy behavior when you go through any kind of loss. People grieve in different ways – some cry more than others. Express your feelings in whatever way feels best for you. Veterinarians and their staffs also feel very sad about the ending of a pet's life. Hopefully, your veterinarian will be able to share your sadness. Talk to your veterinarian about this issue, if it is a problem for you.

Fear of What People Will Think If You Don't Cry.
"Will people think I don't care about my pet if I don't cry when my pet is euthanized?"

Women are "supposed" to cry easily when they are sad. Men aren't supposed to cry easily. If you don't want to cry in front of others, it does not mean that you're not grieving. You may prefer to cry in private, or not to cry at all. And that is okay. Just try to find some other way to release your grief so it doesn't stay trapped inside you.

Fear of Loss of a Close Relationship.
"I will no longer have a child, best friend, or partner."
"What about the emptiness in my life after my pet is no longer in it?"

You will need support from others as you readjust to a changed way of life without your pet. Ask yourself who else you have in your life for support. This could be people and/or other pets. Dealing with emptiness in your life is dealt with under *Needs for Support* in Chapter 17.

Fear of Loss of Part of Your Identity.
"I think I will be a different person after my pet dies."

You are correct. The death of your pet can trigger an identity crisis. In your relationship with your pet you play certain roles. Your pet reflects back to you your identity as a caregiver, a parent, a partner, or a friend. The death of your pet ends the reflection of this part of your identity. Therefore, a redefinition of yourself will have to take place. Truly, after the death of your pet, you will not be the same person you were when your pet was alive. In time, you will develop relationships with other people or other pets to help with these role losses.

Fear of Ending a Relationship.
"It feels so frightening to think of this relationship ending."

This is a fear that will bring up memories of other relationship endings in your life. How have your close past relationships ended? Did the relationships end through death? If not, who left the relationship – you or the other person? If you left, you probably felt a sense of control. If the other person left you, you may have felt powerless, helpless, and angry.

It is important for you to feel you have some power and control when a relationship ends. Read the section under *Control* in Chapter 17, and *Helplessness* in this chapter to decide what you can do to overcome that helpless feeling and regain a sense of control.

Fear of Abuse of Power.
*"How can I plan the death of such a close friend who trusts me
and is so dependent on me?"*
"I feel like I am killing my best friend."

As a pet owner, you have the responsibility of authority over your pet,
even extending to life and death issues. But you are afraid of abusing
that power. Because euthanasia feels like murder, you may feel you
are abusing your power. Do you see yourself as a murderer, and your
pet as a victim?

The authority or power issue can be a very complicated issue for
anyone who was abused in any way by a parent or another adult
authority figure in childhood. If you fear you are using your authority
in an abusive way to euthanize your pet, you will need to make new
connections in your thought patterns between the concepts of killing
as a power abuse, and killing as rescue from pain. Refer to the power
abuse discussion in Chapter 6 for a detailed analysis of this fear.

*TAKE ACTION. Face your fears. Understand what you are afraid
of, and formulate a plan of action to deal with your fears.*

Anger

It is understandable you would feel angry when you are hurting so
deeply, and your needs are not being met. Which of the following are
making you angry?

♦ You are going through a difficult ending to one of the most
   meaningful relationships in your life.

♦ You are watching your loved pet slowly deteriorate.

♦ You have to make difficult and tricky medical decisions.

♦ You have to consider ending your pet's life, which goes
   against everything you believe in.

♦ You have to make decisions, when you don't like any of the options.

♦ You feel backed into a corner, trapped, with no way out.

♦ You think no one else could ever understand.

♦ You are furious at your impending loss.

♦ You are irritated at your pet for putting you through this.

When your anger comes out, it may be directed at an innocent party. There may be times when you are angry with your veterinarian, and blame him for something. Or, maybe you will yell at a family member for some minor reason. You may direct anger toward yourself, and blame yourself for doing something that might have caused the death. You may be angry at another pet who is still healthy.

Anger at God. If you have a religious faith, you may feel angry with God for allowing this to happen to you and your pet. You might ask why it couldn't happen to someone else's unloved pet. Others have questioned why God allows bad things to happen. You might want to look at H.S. Kushner's book, *When Bad Things Happen To Good People*, (New York:Schocken, 1981), as you struggle with these questions.

TO THINK ABOUT. What are you angry about? How does your anger come out?

Expressing Your Anger. Anger may frighten you, especially if you have previously witnessed anger that was out of control and destructive. But anger can be released in ways that are safe, appropriate, and liberating. Anger, appropriately expressed, can be a powerful, healing force. Anger, hidden inside, can cause many physical symptoms, including headaches, ulcers and eating disorders. So, take time to identify, feel, and express your anger.

Let's talk about some ways you can constructively release your anger. Anger stirs up a great deal of energy inside you. You want to stay in control of that energy. How can you discharge your anger energy? Physical activities such as walking, swimming, biking, even pounding your pillow, or chopping wood, are excellent ways to release anger. In my office I have a beanbag chair and a baseball bat that people can pound on to get their anger out. Talking about your frustrations with a sympathetic friend is usually helpful. Screaming and letting out feelings in a room or car where you won't be heard is a good release for some. Writing out angry feelings, and even tearing up the writing, can be a help for those who like to write.

After their pet dies, some people like to channel their anger by doing something constructive to help others. Some pet owners come to my pet loss support group as a way to help others after their own grief has subsided. Can you warn others of some danger to pets? Can you write about your experiences to help other pet owners?

TAKE ACTION. **Decide how you will constructively release your anger.**

Helplessness

It is common to feel initially helpless in the face of serious illness and approaching death, or your inability to find a home for a pet you can no longer keep. A lack of knowledge, and the resulting feelings of loss-of-control, will intensify your sense of helplessness. Although you can't cure disease, give back youth to an elderly pet, or find a suitable adoptive home, you have more power and control than you may realize.

♦ Things look worse when you look at everything at the same time. Take one thing at a time, one day at a time, and sometimes even one hour at a time.

♦ Figure out what you can control, and what circumstances are out of your control. (See *Control Needs* in Chapter 17).

♦ Gather information and make decisions.

TAKE ACTION. **Plan what you will do to avoid feeling helpless.**

Embarrassment

Are you ashamed of your intense feelings about you pet's approaching death and euthanasia? Have insensitive people made cruel comments that leave you feeling there must be something wrong with your being so upset?

I hope, after reading this book, you will understand better why you are having such inner turmoil in reaction to approaching death and euthanasia of your pet. Talk with people who understand what you are going through. Keep away from people who don't understand your feelings, or ask them to respect the fact that you are grieving, even if they don't understand why.

Judy told a coworker who belittled her grief when her cat, Casey, died, that the coworker had children, but she (Judy) had no children. Casey had been her child, so she was grieving the death of her child.

TAKE ACTION. Decide what you will you say if someone belittles or doesn't understand your grief.

Loneliness

You will feel loncly and incomplete during your pet's illness and approaching death. Loneliness is a signal that you need emotional connection with someone with whom you can share your thoughts, feelings and experiences.

Where can you find other animal lovers who will understand what you are going through? In Chapter 17 under *Support Needs* there are suggestions for places to connect with other animal lovers. Even an activity such as walking a neighbor's pet around the neighborhood can be helpful when you are without one of your own. Conversations start easily when someone responds to the pet with you while you are out for a walk. Try attending a cat, dog, or horse show, or club meeting. Some bereaved pet owners tell me they volunteer at various animal shelters, humane societies, or local zoos. Use your imagination to think of ways to meet other animal lovers.

TAKE ACTION. What will you do when you feel lonely?

Depression

Depression is a feeling of sadness, hopelessness and pessimism which is usually present to some extent while you are grieving a loss. It can also recur on the anniversary date of a loss. Depressed people blame themselves for anything that goes wrong, even those things over which they have no control. Symptoms of depression include: anxiety, irritability, appetite and sleep problems, poor concentration, forgetfulness, and indecisiveness.

Avoid the use of alcohol or nonprescription drugs to help overcome depression, as they may increase your low moods. Adequate sleep, good nutrition and exercise all help combat depression. If you think your depression is lasting too long, obtain professional counseling, or talk to your family physician.

TAKE ACTION. *What will you do to fight depression?*
Which feelings discussed in this chapter are you having the most trouble dealing with? How do you plan to express these feelings?

CHAPTER 17

Your Pet Isn't the Only One With Needs

The euthanasia experience is emotionally exhausting. How often, when you are thinking about choosing death for your pet, does attention focus only on what is good for your pet, leaving you and your needs out of the picture? The focus of this book is on you – the pet owner, and the decision-maker. *From the moment you start thinking about choosing death for your pet, there are two patients in this drama – you and your pet.* Your pet has medical needs, but you are under tremendous stress, and also have many needs. Let's discuss some of the needs you, as a pet owner, have at this difficult time:

Stress Reduction Needs

You probably have been feeling a great deal of stress since you started considering choosing death for your pet. Take the following steps to cope with stress effectively:

Monitor Your Stress Level. Symptoms of *physical stress* include: headaches, stomachaches, muscle tension, fatigue, overeating, drug or alcohol abuse, appetite loss, constipation, diarrhea, rapid heartbeat, insomnia, nightmares.

Symptoms of *psychological stress* include: forgetfulness, poor concentration, irritability, restlessness, hyperactivity, anger, anxiety, crying, depression.

TAKE ACTION. Go back through the lists of physical and psychological stress and circle each symptom you are experiencing. How many symptoms did you circle? How frequent is each of the symptoms you identified?
If you weren't aware of when you were feeling stress, plan to start "listening" to you body for symptoms such as headaches or stomach upsets that tell you when you are under stress.

Identify The Sources of Your Stress. Do you know what factors are causing your stress? How much have the following raised your stress level?

♦ Watching a healthy pet deteriorate into an unwell pet.
♦ Caring for an ill pet who presents feeding, medication, or incontinence problems.
♦ Considering an euthanasia decision that you don't want to make.
♦ Life changes that the illness and death of your pet bring to you.
♦ Lack of the emotional support you once received from your pet.
♦ Lack of understanding and support from people in your life.
♦ Financial strain of medical care, burial or cremation, or even mental health counseling for yourself.

Are You Experiencing Stress Overload? If you have other anxiety-provoking problems in your life at this time, you may be experiencing stress overload. Your own poor health, a job loss, a job change, a divorce, an aged parent, a move, or a child leaving home, are examples of additional stressful problems that you might be coping with at this time.

Each person has his own individual breaking point. When you reach your "breaking point," you will not be able to tolerate any additional stress without it seriously affecting your mental health.

TAKE ACTION. What sources of stress do you have? Do you have some kinds of stress that are not included in the above list? Make a list of your sources of stress.

Plan Time For Stress Reduction Activities. Stress can be hazardous to your health. Research seems to indicate a link between stress and many physical ailments such as tension headaches, high blood pressure, cancer, and heart disease. A healthy lifestyle that includes the following will help you cope with stress:

♦ Regular physical exercise such as walking, biking, or swimming, will help you discharge the negative energy that builds up inside your body when you are under stress.

♦ Regular, well-balanced meals will help fight depression.

♦ Adequate sleep and relaxation will refresh you, and give you energy to care for your pet and make decisions.

♦ Lower your standards. It's okay if your house isn't immaculate right now. Don't expect to put in a top performance on the job. You won't have the energy to do as much as you usually do. Don't add to your stress by trying to keep up with all your usual routines.

♦ Use music to reduce your stress. Slow, soothing music will calm your nerves.

♦ Try the "six-second cure." When you feel under stress, close your eyes, and relax your facial muscles. Visualize a smile spreading across your face and up to your eyes. Take a deep breath, and imagine you are inhaling through the bottoms of your feet, and bringing air up though your legs all the way into your lungs. Exhale, with a deep sigh, and imagine the air flowing back down through your legs and out of your body. Let your jaw, tongue and shoulders go limp.

TAKE ACTION. Is there anything you can do to help alleviate your stressful situations? Maybe you need to find another supportive person to talk with, or to set a limit on how much time you can devote to caring for your dying pet.

Control Needs

Just thinking about euthanasia may leave you with a helpless, out-of-control feeling. Let's take a realistic look at what your predicament is. You have to figure out a way to:

Feel Some Control Over Events. When you are in a situation that leaves you feelings helpless, start looking around to see what you can do – what decisions you can make, what actions you can take that will give you a feeling of control. Let's take a minute to identify what factors are out of your control, and what you *can* control as you and your pet face this experience together.

Circumstances That Are Out of Your Control:
♦ Your pet's illness, aging, or temperament problem .
♦ Bodily changes that accompanies disease or old age.
♦ The administration of some of the medical procedures.
♦ The existence of your painful grief feelings.

Circumstances That Are Under Your Control. Decisions and reactions that are under your control include:

♦ Your decisions about your pet's medical treatment.
♦ The time, place, and way your pet's life will end.
♦ What you want to do for your pet as part of letting go.
♦ How you want to say goodbye to your pet.
♦ Whether you want to be present when your pet dies.
♦ What you do with your pet's body after death.
♦ The way you express your feelings.
♦ How well you care for yourself when under stress.
♦ The ways you pay tribute to your pet's life.

It's important to remember that you are not in control of your pet's ultimate fate, the aging process or bodily disease. When it is time for your pet to die – one way or another it will happen.

You can be in control of the way and time things happen. If you want, you can be the agent in helping to bring about death in a more gentle way and with less suffering than nature offers. Remember that if you choose death for an ill pet, you are not truly the cause of death, you are only the agent.

As you move through this experience you will be working on increasing your feelings of control in three different areas: psychological, physical, and social.

Psychologically you will gain a sense of control as you acknowledge and deal with your feelings. You won't feel so helpless as you face death.

Physically you will feel better as you learn what to expect, and take actions to feel more in control and reduce your stress.

Socially surround yourself with friends and professionals who can support you and validate your feelings. Stay away from people who don't understand. Let others care for you.

So, acknowledge your anxiety about the parts of this situation that are out of your control. But, even more important, tell yourself, "I'll handle it. I have the ability to move beyond my fears, to make decisions and to handle this situation." At first you may not believe yourself when you say this. You may even have to pretend for a while. But keep giving yourself this positive message. You might even want to put up a sign "I'LL HANDLE IT" where you can see it frequently.

The good news is that each decision you make, each action you take as you move through this experience, will prove to you that you are handling it. As you deal with events, you will feel more powerful and in control in this intimidating situation. *Your feelings of helplessness and despair will decrease in proportion to the amount of actions you take and decisions you make.*

TAKE ACTION. Shut your eyes and visualize yourself making decisions and taking actions that leave you feeling in control.

Responsible Decision-Making Needs

When you join your life with your pet's, you don't take a formal vow of responsibility. But you do have an obligation of responsibility to your pet, for better or worse. Your responsibility is to provide loving care, training, grooming, medical care, and, finally, a peaceful death for your pet. Because of the responsibility that comes with pet ownership, it is up to you to make this decision about your pet's death. It is not a decision for anyone else to make. It is *your* decision.

You may find it difficult to think clearly enough to make decisions while you are grieving. But you have a responsibility to yourself to feel your feelings as you make this decision for your pet. Remember that decision-making will help you feel some control over what is happening, and thereby stabilize you in the midst of overwhelming emotions. Chapter 14 outlines steps to help you make decisions you will feel comfortable about.

TO THINK ABOUT. Remember that the final decision of whether to choose death for your pet is not a decision you make to satisfy anyone except yourself and your pet.

Grief Needs

You are the only one who knows what the loss of your pet means to you. You are the only one who knows how badly it hurts. Acknowledge and express your pain and grief. Don't try to avoid it or put it off. Until you do so, you will not heal from your loss.

Each of us expresses grief in different ways. Possible ways to express your grief include: tears, words, music, art work, or any other way that feels right to you. Don't let anyone tell you how to release your grief. And don't criticize anyone close to you who grieves differently than you.

TO THINK ABOUT. How well are you meeting your needs to acknowledge and express your grief?

Support Needs

One of the most helpful ways you can deal with your feelings during the euthanasia experience is by talking with other supportive people. You have the need:

For Reassurance. You need to have people tell you that you made the right decision. If you wonder whether your grief feelings are normal, compare feelings with others who have been through the euthanasia of a pet. Chances are, you will find that your grief feelings are typical.

For Respect. Do your family and friends respect your grief, even if they don't like pets? If you have someone in your life who doesn't understand why you are grieving so deeply about your pet, tell them that you want them to respect *the fact you are grieving*, even if they don't understand *why* you are in so much pain. It is possible that friends may not recognize your intense suffering, and you may be too ashamed of your feelings to easily talk to people about what you are going through.

As you face this sorrowful experience, I hope you have family or friends who are supportive and can comfort you. Maybe it would be helpful for you to stop for a minute and think about your support system. Who do you feel comfortable talking with about your feelings: friends, family members, clergy, neighbors, your veterinarian, your veterinarian's staff, your pet's groomer, your pet shop owner? Anyone else?

TAKE ACTION. Write down supportive people's names and phone numbers and put them by your phone.

Pet Loss Support Group. Supportive people who understand what you are going through because they have been through a similar experience are most likely to understand. In a pet loss support group, you will find people who come together to share experiences, and support each other as they talk about the death of their pets. The very thing that makes you feel isolated in your life – the loss of your pet – is your ticket of admission to a pet loss support group. If you have no supportive human friends, ask your veterinarian if he knows of a pet loss support group, or consult the Delta Society at PO Box 1080, Renton, WA. 98057-1080, PH; (206) 226-7357, to see whether there is a pet loss support group in your area.

If you locate a pet loss support group, you may want to ask questions to find out about the group before you attend a meeting. Is there a group leader? Is the group leader a trained mental health professional (social worker, psychologist, etc.)? Is there a charge for the group? How long will the group session last? How many people attend? How often does the group meet?

A group with a trained leader is preferable to one without a leader. The leader will ensure that the group has structure, and everyone has the opportunity to talk, if they want. A trained mental health professional can best help group members express and deal with overwhelming feelings.

The Internet. Computer technology has given us the World Wide Web – a new way to connect with supportive pet lovers from all over the world when we are grieving. Specific sites of interest change, so use one of the many search facilities to locate web sites related to keywords such as *pets, animals, dog, cat, horse, bird,* and *rainbow bridge.*

On the Internet you will find pet grief support pages, and a weekly Monday Evening Candle Ceremony for animal lovers who are grieving the death of a pet. There are places to swap animal stories, and obtain support and information about pet loss.

Individual Counseling. If the idea of pet euthanasia leaves you feeling too overwhelmed, you may decide to talk individually with a trained professional counselor. Short-term counseling can be very helpful during the euthanasia experience. A counselor can provide objectivity and a sense of direction as you make decisions and express your feelings. If the euthanasia decision has triggered other upsetting memories or abuse of power issues, a counselor can help you deal with these. The Appendix lists counseling resources.

You can best help your pet if you take care of yourself. I am constantly amazed by pet owners who tell me they have spent hundreds, and even thousands, of dollars on medical care for their pet, but refuse to spend any money on themselves for pet loss counseling.

TAKE ACTION. Give yourself permission to care for yourself as well as you care for your pet.

Time Needs

Time is one of your most important needs right now. Unless you have a crisis situation, the euthanasia decision is not a decision to make quickly because it is not reversible. Also, it takes time to move through the various steps of the euthanasia experience as outlined in this book.

You have the need to give yourself time to:

♦ Accept the reality of your pet's approaching death.
♦ Deal with your thoughts and feelings about this painful experience.

- ◆ Talk with others who have had a similar experience.
- ◆ Gather information and make decisions.
- ◆ Do all that you want to for your pet.
- ◆ Say goodbye to your pet.
- ◆ Heal from your grief – be patient because this takes time.

TAKE ACTION. Give yourself time to deal with all your thoughts and feelings, and to take whatever actions you need to take in connection with your pet's approaching death. Give yourself time to heal following your pet's death.

Forgiving Your Pet For Dying Needs

It is difficult to forgive our pet's body for wearing out and dying. Somehow, we each secretly hope that, in the case of our pet, an exception will be made. Our pet will figure out a way to outwit nature, and be with us the rest of our lives. The amount of shock we feel when we realize our pet's body is dying, tells us how much we deny the natural process of death of the body. Most pet owners have made plans several years into the future, even with elderly pets, hoping they and their pets will be together for many years to come.

As quickly as you can overcome your shock at the approaching death of your pet's body, you need to forgive the body for dying. It is through this acceptance and forgiveness of bodily death that you can find the strength and courage to face the end of your earthly relationship with your pet.

TAKE ACTION. Accept and forgive your pet's body for dying.

Need to Formulate a Philosophy About What Happens After Death for Animals

The death of the body raises the most fundamental questions of existence for you to consider. What happens after death for an animal? Does an animal have a soul that lives on after death? Will you be with your pet in some other dimension after you both die? Let's look at how other animal lovers have answered these difficult questions.

Are animals really inferior to man? In *The Outermost House*, Henry Beston writes that animals should not be compared to man. They are neither "brethren" nor "underlings", and have many capabilities that are actually superior to man's. He refers to them as "other nations" who are "fellow prisoners" with us here on earth.

The idea that there is no "after life" for animals, can be distressing. But most animal lovers, including James Herriot, feel there must be a special place where pets will be rewarded for the love and devotion they have given to their human friends. In *The Best of James Herriot*, a dying woman asks James Herriot whether her animals have souls, and will be with her after death. He replies that animals are better off than many humans because they feel "love, loyalty and gratitude." He concludes by assuring the woman that her pets will go where ever she is going when she dies.

Finally, the most convincing reason I've heard for pets going to Heaven is: "It wouldn't be Heaven without them." (Author unknown)

Helpful Resources: Animal communicator, Penelope Smith's reassuring audiotape: *Animal Death: A Spiritual Journey* can be ordered from Pegasus Publications, Phone: 1-800-356-9315. Also request a list of Penelope's books and quarterly newsletter, *Species Link*. Another book, *The Souls of Animals*, by Gary Kowalski, Stillpoint Publishing, 1991, might be helpful.

What Other Needs Do You Have?

Make a list. You will find that if you take the time to understand and meet your needs, your stress level will diminish greatly, and you will have more energy and a better sense of well-being.

PART IV

AFTER THE EUTHANASIA

CHAPTER 18

A Pet Loss Support Group Discusses Burial and Cremation Options

The Pet Loss Support Group had gathered for their regular monthly meeting that August morning. The meeting opened with people in the circle introducing themselves by telling the group briefly about the pet they were grieving, and how well they were coping.

At the previous meeting, the group had decided to talk about what they had done with their pet's body or ashes following death. The leader opened the discussion by stating that rituals are helpful in resolving our grief feelings when someone dies. Many rituals revolve around what we do with a pet's body after death, and ceremonies that take place in connection with final arrangements.

Rituals give us an opportunity to express our grief, a formal way to commemorate the significance of the relationship with our pet, and a way to mark an ending to that relationship. A pet's grave or ashes help us face the reality of death because they are a constant reminder that our pet has, indeed, died.

Marie started the discussion by showing the group a collage. When her beloved Yorkie, Abby, died, Marie had the owner of a local frame shop help her design this collage, which was set in a very deep wooden frame. Included in the collage were a tiny, pink, heart-shaped box containing Abby's ashes, a picture of Abby, and a sock that had been Abby's favorite toy. Marie hung the collage on her living room wall. She found it to be unexpectedly therapeutic, because whenever someone asked her about the collage, she had a chance to reminisce about Abby.

Jeanene, a young mother with three small children, said after her Dalmatian, Blaze, was euthanized due to complications of old age, she kept his ashes in her home for a few months. Then, on a lovely fall day, she and her family went to a lake in the country, and had a little ceremony as they scattered Blaze's ashes where he used to love to run and chase rabbits and squirrels.

Leslie, a divorced teacher in her late 20's, said her cat, Magic, died from feline leukemia. After he was cremated, the thought occurred to her that Magic used to love to sit in the sun in front of her flower garden. She mixed Magic's ashes in the flower garden that spring, so the flowers would reminded her of Magic.

Leslie's neighbor buried her pets' ashes at the base of a flowering tree or shrub in her large yard. The tree she chose was determined by what she wanted to remember about each pet's unique appearance, personality, etc.

Kim, who was attending the group for the first time, sadly told the group about the euthanasia four days earlier of her horse, Arizona. Kim had decided to have only Arizona's heart, head, and hooves cremated because the cost of cremating the entire horse was prohibitive. She scattered some of his ashes along a favorite trail where they used to ride, and kept the rest of the ashes in a trophy she and Arizona had won in competition. She buried his horseshoes and some hair from his mane and tail near her favorite trail, also.

Marge recalled that, after her Pekingese, Chou Chou, died, she had been fortunate enough to travel to China, the ancestral home of that Oriental breed. To the ancient Chinese, the Pekingese was considered to be a sacred dog, so Marge placed some of Chou Chou's ashes in a sacred garden in China.

Betty told the group she was checking into a cemetery she had heard about that was supposed to accept the ashes of both pets and people. She wanted to bury her pets' ashes there as they died. Her plan was that, after death, her own ashes would also be buried there. Betty said she had learned that the only cemetery in the United States that accepts burial of bodies of both pets and humans is the Bonheur Memorial Park in Elkridge, Maryland. Pets and their owners can be buried in adjacent plots in this cemetery.

Sharla told Betty that she was saving all the ashes of her extensive family of dogs. Her plan was that the ashes of her "kids" would be put into her coffin and buried with her when she dies.

John and Daisy, a couple in their 70s, said that long before their first poodle, Fluffer, died in 1982, they had decided to bury her in a pet cemetery because she was like a special child to them. There is also a stone inscribed with the name of their present poodle, Autumn Blaze, waiting in the cemetery. John and Daisy said they are comforted by frequent visits to the graves of Fluffer.

The leader noted that there are over 500 cemeteries in this country which accept a variety of pets, such as ducks, rabbits, snakes, goats, gerbils, llamas, and, of course, dogs and cats. Several of the cemeteries are reserved just for horses. Local pet cemeteries are listed in the yellow pages of the phone book under *Pet Cemeteries and Crematories.*

If you have special pet cemetery needs, contact: *The International Association of Pet Cemeteries. Phone: 1-800-952-5541.*

Denise said she had always buried her pets in her backyard. She could visit their graves as many times a day as she wanted to, and could plant flowers and trees near their graves. This is usually not permitted in a pet cemetery. Also, it was a lot cheaper than a pet cemetery. She either buried the pet in a sealed container, or buried it three feet down in the ground so no animal would dig it up. Her biggest concern about back yard burial was if she someday sold her house and moved away, what would happen to her pets' graves?

Several group members said it comforted them to bury favorite toys, collars, blankets, and clothing, with their pets. Many had expressed their grief by holding some type of funeral service, complete with eulogies and poems they had written about their pets. Clergy had read appropriate scriptures at some of the funerals.

The group leader summarized the available options:

Burial and Cremation Options

Whether to Choose Burial or Cremation?
Burial will return your pet's body to nature. Some religions are opposed to cremation.

Cremation allows you to keep your pet's ashes with you. During cremation in a large oven, the soft parts of the body melt away. The ashes that remain, called "cremains," are actually small bone pieces. Cremation is a quick, clean process, and is less expensive than burial in a pet cemetery.

Burial Options: Home burial, or pet cemetery in an individual plot, or a mass burial.

Advantages of a Pet Cemetery: A pet cemetery provides a permanent, peaceful resting place. The grave is dug for you. Caskets and headstones are available. There is a perpetual care option, and there may be a chapel and viewing room.

Disadvantage of a Pet Cemetery: Cost. This is the highest priced option. If you move, you will not be near your pet's grave.

Advantages of Home Burial: It's easy and inexpensive. It's nearby, so it's easy to visit your pet's grave daily. You can plant flowers and trees on the grave.

Disadvantages of Home Burial: It's illegal in many places.
It will be difficult to dig the grave for a large pet, or when the ground is frozen in winter. What happens to the grave if you move?

Advantages and Disadvantages of Mass Burial: It's inexpensive and uncomplicated. But there is no grave to visit, and there is a lack of rituals that help with grief resolution.

Burial Decisions:

Whether to choose home burial, pet cemetery burial, or mass burial? To consider: Is home burial legal in your town? If so, are you planning to live in the same place for the next few years? How much can you afford to spend for burial? Do you want an individual grave that you can visit?

What is the cost of the various forms of burial? Home burial is the least expensive, with the only cost being for a sealed container, or grave marker, if you choose them. Mass burial costs vary, but are considerably less expensive than a private plot in a pet cemetery. A private pet cemetery burial starts at $350, and can go to thousands of dollars. Fees are charged for the purchase of the plot and perpetual care, the casket, sometimes a cement vault, a grave marker, and the opening and closing the grave.

Who will transport your pet's body to the pet cemetery?
You can. However, if you find it upsetting, your veterinarian or the pet cemetery can also arrange for this service.

Cremation Options: Individual cremation or mass cremation.

Cremation Decisions:

Whether to choose single or mass cremation? Do you want your pet's ashes returned to you? If so, choose single cremation.

How much will it cost? Cost is determined by the weight of the pet. An individual cremation is $75 and up. A mass cremation is less.

Who will transport the pet's body to the crematorium? Your veterinarian can arrange for this service, if you find it distasteful.

How long will cremation take? Usually a matter of hours. The ashes will be ready when they cool – probably the next day.

What to do with the ashes? You can keep ashes in a special container at home, scatter them in a special place, bury them in a special place, or save them for later burial with you.

TAKE ACTION. Make final arrangements for your pet before its death. What you choose to do with your pet's body will depend on your personal preferences, your religious views, cost, and your degree of attachment to your pet. Do what feels right for you to express your love for your pet.

CHAPTER 19

Tips For Adjusting to Life After Your Pet's Death

Following the death of your pet, you stand at the threshold of a new and altered lifestyle. As you enter this new phase of your life, in addition to expressing your grief, you will need to be creative in dealing with the challenge of change. How will you use the time and energy you used to share with your pet? How will you keep your pet's memory alive? How will you find support for yourself? Will you get another pet? If so, when?

Healthy Grief Responses. The first thing you will notice after the death of your pet are what we call "healthy grief responses." Common healthy grief responses feel terrible and slow you down. They include: crying spells, depression, mood swings between feeling tired and feeling hyperactive, loss of energy, lack of concentration, forgetfulness, anxiety, anger, and guilt. Your body often reacts by giving you headaches, stomachaches, or catching a cold. You may lose your appetite, or overeat. You may be unable to sleep, or have nightmares or insomnia. In time, these healthy grief responses will decrease, as you express your grief.

Unhealthy Grief Responses. Basically, unhealthy grief responses are attempts to cope with grief by keeping busy to avoid the painful grief feelings listed above. Some people distract themselves with compulsively endless work (employment or housework), or other forms of activities such as excessive shopping, overeating, exercising, gambling, drinking too much alcohol, or drug abuse.

The problem with the unhealthy grief responses is that they suppress grief so that grief feelings are not expressed. Also, they may have additional harmful side effects on your body, or your finances. Unexpressed grief will remain in the unconscious, sometimes for years, waiting to be expressed. If you think you are trapped in unhealthy grief responses, you need to work on learning to express your grief.

Ways To Express Your Grief. Throughout the book, we've discussed various ways to release the energy that grief stirs up inside your body. Crying, one of the most effective ways to discharge grief, is not easy for everyone. Other ways to express grief include talking to others or talking into a tape recorder. Some find exercise, such as walking, helpful.

Writing can help to release grief. Write a thank you letter to your pet for all the joy he brought into your life. Write a letter to your pet saying goodbye. Write a letter from your pet to you, answering your letters, or telling you what you think your pet would tell you to help you get through your grief. Some people write poems or short stories about their pet. Others keep a daily journal of their thoughts and feelings about their pet.

Rituals help you express grief and validate your loss. What rituals are available to help a grieving pet owner? Rituals include actions such as saying goodbye to your pet's body, or having a funeral or memorial service for your pet. Attending a pet loss support group is also considered a ritual to help express grief.

Remember that, as you release your grief, and slowly move beyond it, you will not forget your pet. Letting go of grief does not mean you will let go of memories. If you are worried about the possibility of forgetting your pet, start to build a memory file about your life with your pet. Include pictures and writings, letters, poems, and stories about your pet.

While you are grieving, take care of yourself. Take time off work, if you need to. You are entitled to grieve as much for your pet as you would if a person had died. You do not need to apologize or offer explanations to anyone about why you are feeling so upset. It is your own personal business.

How Much Grief? Many people are surprised that they cry more when a pet dies than they did when a relative died. If questioned, these same people usually realize that they had a much closer emotional relationship with their pet than with their relative. Also, there may be less ambivalence in a relationship with a pet. A pet does not threaten or challenge us the way another person can.

How Long Does Grief Last? Grief seems to go on forever when you are mourning. The length of time grief lasts varies with each person. Just tell yourself that, as you express each feeling, and take care of yourself, you are moving through the process of grief toward feeling better. There will be times when you feel better, and times when you plunge back down into the grief again. But, slowly, the times of feeling better should come more frequently, and last longer. Give yourself credit for small accomplishments, such as when you can walk by the pet food aisle in the grocery store without getting tearful, or think about your pet without crying. If you don't feel any better after a month or two, think about getting some professional help.

How To Deal With Those Who Are Not Sympathetic To Your Grief. There will be people who won't understand, and who are insensitive enough to make rude remarks about the expression of your grief. Remember that you are entitled to grieve for your pet as much as you need to, for as long as you need to. You are entitled to respect for the fact you are grieving, even if people don't understand why you feel so upset.

Some people will respond to a request for respect for your grief. Some won't. Try to stay away from anyone who doesn't understand, be they coworkers, best friends, or family members. They will only make your grief worse by their lack of understanding. Members of a pet loss support group will help you by validating your grief and your right to express it.

Change Your Routine. Keeping the same routine will constantly remind you of your pet who did many of those activities with you. So, see how creative you can be in finding different ways to do your daily activities.

If breakfast time reminds you of feeding your pet, go out to a restaurant, invite a friend over, or join a friend elsewhere for breakfast. Eat in a different room, or a different spot in the same room. If you always read your newspaper in the same location with your pet at your feet or on your shoulder, go somewhere else to read your newspaper. Even leave the house, and read your newspaper in the park or at the library.

If you were in the habit of walking your pet, try walking at a different time of day, or invite a neighbor to walk with you. Take a different route than you used to walk.

Recognize that, as hard as you try to change your routine, certain places will trigger sudden tears for awhile, such as driving by your veterinarian's office.

Finding New Ways to Use Your Time and Energy. What will you do with the time and energy you used to direct toward activities with your pet? Check out the adult evening classes at the local high school or art center. Did you ever want to learn to dance, improve your cooking skills, learn pottery-making, astrology, genealogy, car repair, how to use a computer, or skydive ? *Now is the time to sign up for a challenging new activity that you know nothing about.* As an extra bonus, you might also make some new friends while attending the class.

Highly recommended among the list of new activities is connecting with other animal lovers either on the Internet, or in person at a pet loss support group. Other animal lovers will understand what you are going through. If there is no local pet loss group, consider starting one. Some SPCAs, veterinarians, or professional counselors who like pets might be willing to help you get one going.

While you are looking for new activities, don't get so busy that you hide from your memories, happy or sad. Set aside times to remember your pet and to grieve. Purposely visiting places you and your pet went together will help you remember and mourn. Perhaps you will feel especially close to your pet at those times. Work on a list of happy memories about your pet, and keep adding to it as time goes by. Read it to the pet loss support group. It will probably stir up a discussion of other pet owners' happy memories with their pets.

Keeping Your Pet's Memory Alive. This is another area where you can be especially creative. Doing something to keep your pet's memory alive is part of working through your grief.

Suzanne wears a silver pin that has a place for a picture. Instead of a picture, she put a lock of her dog, Zack's, hair in the pin. She also has made a pillow stuffed with the hair of her current dog, Abby, as a future memory symbol of that dog.

Nellie said it helped her feel close to her deceased dog, Joe, when she carried his leash in her pocket. Others feel comforted when they carry small pet toys, or even the pet's ashes, in pockets or purses as symbolic reminders of their pets. Some pet owners have their pet's paw print put in clay.

Mickey found a small stuffed toy cat with a ceramic head that looked very much like her cat, Blackberry, who had died recently. The toy cat comforted her as she carried it with her from place to place. She, also, had a portrait painted from Blackberry's favorite photo.

Wanda and Tony and their children framed a collage of pictures of their deceased dog, Reese, together with his AKC registration paper, to hang on their wall. Reese's collar hangs on the corner of the picture frame, and his dog tags have been made into a key chain.

Flowers and trees planted at the grave site of a beloved pet, or even just planted in memory of the pet, can help keep the memory alive.

Financial donations, given in your pet's name to animal-related charities, are a loving tribute to the memory of your pet. Seeing your deceased pet's name listed, because you contributed to a worthy cause, can help you connect with your pet's loving presence once again.

Your support of other pet owners who are grieving the loss of a pet can be one of the most wonderful tributes you can make to your pet. Many pet owners attend pet loss support groups to support others, even when their own grief has diminished in intensity. Giving your grieving friend a copy of this book would be a supportive tribute.

Getting Through the Holidays. Holidays seem to deepen grief because they remind you of how your life changed with the death of your pet. It doesn't work to try to forget your pet and push grief out of the holiday. Light a candle in memory of your pet. Put a wreath on the pet's grave. Donate money or a gift to a worthy cause in memory of your pet. Give money or pet food to a local SPCA for a special holiday treat for the animals there.

At Christmas time, Trisha gave a carrot to each of her remaining horses as a present from her horse, Molly, who had died that year. Doug had a special Christmas tree ornament designed in the shape of a parakeet, with Blue's name on it, so his deceased parakeet would be included in his Christmas thoughts. He created a little ceremony to accompany the hanging of Blue's ornament on the tree. Deidre has a Christmas tree ornament for each of her 12 cats with their name on it. Her plan is that each ornament will continue to be a reminder of the part each cat has played in her life, even after the death of the cat.

Be kind to yourself. The holidays will eventually pass. Try to be with others, if you can. It will help you feel less alone. If you have a chance to visit away from home for the holidays, do so, if it feels right.

How Long To Wait Before Getting Another Pet. When a pet dies, there is often a feeling of wanting to rush out and find another pet to fill the empty void. It's better to wait awhile before starting the search for a new pet for the following reasons:

❖ You will probably be trying to find a pet that looks and acts like your former pet. But every pet is unique, so you will end up feeling frustrated. Even if you find a pet that looks similar, be aware that it won't act the same. You could end up resenting the new pet for the ways it differs from your former one.

❖ The depression that accompanies grief may leave you with little energy to look for, choose, and train a new pet. Wait until you have the energy to search out the right pet, and train it.

❖ If you decide to adopt your next pet from the SPCA, remember that while you are actively grieving, you may find it difficult to look at animals who may be euthanized within a short time. I have known people who became more depressed than they already were by visiting the SPCA too early in the grief process.

If you are the type of person who gets a lot of emotional support from a pet, you might want to consider having two pets, so that you won't be without any pets when one dies.

Some pet owners want a new pet, but are upset at the thought of going through the terrible grief when the pet dies. A person who feels this way is still grieving. Grief is the price we pay when a pet or human relationship ends. But most of us would rather face the pain of grief than live a life devoid of any relationships. In time, the pain of grief fades, and the fun of a new pet will look inviting once again.

You may feel you could never love another pet the way you love the deceased pet. It is true you can't duplicate the relationship you had with your pet. But each pet has his own loveable qualities which you will discover when you feel ready to build a new relationship with your next pet.

Some pet owners wonder about getting a new pet when they know their original pet is close to death. I have known pet owners who were surprised at how it rejuvenated an older, or even ill pet, to bring in a new pet. Sometimes the old pet can help train the new pet. However, it does not always work that way. So much depends on the personalities of the pets, and on your life circumstances. Does the original pet feel threatened by a new pet? Do you have time to care for two pets? Does the first pet need a lot of time-consuming care right now? What if the new pet gets sick? Think this out carefully, and proceed cautiously, if you want to try this approach.

Once you have your new pet, remember that it takes time to develop a loving relationship. You can't start a new relationship where you ended the last relationship. But, with time, you will build a new and wonderful relationship with this new member of your family.

How To Meet Needs Your Pet Filled In Your Life. If you decide not to get another pet right now, how can you meet the needs your pet filled in your life? First, you need to identify what needs your pet was meeting for you. Did your pet meet your need for companionship? If so, what will you have to do, or where will you have to go to get that need met? Could you join a club, or a church to participate in their scheduled activities?

Did your pet meet your need for entertainment? Identify what other kinds of entertainment you like. If you don't know, you will have to try various forms of entertainment to see what feels right. Do you like passive forms of entertainment, such as watching movies or sports, or do you like active types of entertainment, such as playing sports or dancing?

Did your pet meet your need to have something to do with your time? How about volunteering to help with a worthy cause, or getting a part-time job?

Did your pet meet your needs to nurture and care for someone? There are many animal organizations and shelters that need people to socialize their animals. You could attend a pet loss support group to help other grieving pet owners. Nursing homes and hospitals, delivering meals-on-wheels, learning to read programs for illiterate adults, Sunday School teacher – all offer ways to help and nurture animals or humans.

Seeking Professional Help. You may feel overwhelmed, or sense a need for some direction or objectivity as you go through grief and readjusting to life after the death of a pet. If you think you are not feeling better as rapidly as you would like, consider talking to a trained professional. *It is a sign of good metal health to reach out for support when you feel the need.*

The next question is: how do you go about locating a pet loss counselor who will understand your feelings? Not all counselors listed in the telephone book yellow pages are sympathetic to pet loss. Ask your veterinarian if he can recommend a good pet loss counselor. If you are fortunate enough to live near a large metropolitan area, you may be near one of the counseling centers associated with a university of veterinary medicine. See the Appendix for a list of these counseling centers.

Your Other Pets. Other pets will go through a grief reaction when an animal friends dies. They usually get depressed, act apathetic, and don't eat very well. Yes, they are grieving, the same as you are. I have heard stories of remaining pets who seem to undergo a personality change, and start acting the way the deceased pet acted.

If you take a pet to the veterinarian for euthanasia, and bring the body back home, show it to the other pets. They need to say goodbye. Pets can become very upset if you take an animal friend to the veterinarian, and they never see their friend again. I have never figured out what to say to my pets, when I show them the dead body of an animal comrade, and they look from the dead pet's body to me with the question in their eyes, "What happened?" But, at least they know their friend is dead.

Don't let your living pets watch you put the deceased pet's body in the ground, if you are doing a home burial. It could be upsetting.

If your most favorite pet dies before less favorite pets, it is possible to feel anger toward the pets who are still alive because they outlived the favorite pet. This doesn't mean you have stopped loving the remaining pet. You would feel terribly upset if one of them died. But anger is part of grief, and it is easy to direct anger toward those nearest to you – your pets.

How To Help a Friend Through Pet Euthanasia.

❖ Try not try to rescue your friend by making decisions for him.

❖ Offer support so your friend will feel empowered to make her own decisions.

❖ Listen, listen, and listen some more.

❖ Beware of forced cheerfulness, that will discourage expression of sad feelings.

❖ Encourage you friend to talk about feelings like sadness, fear and anger.

❖ After your friend makes the euthanasia decision, validate the decision by telling them they did the right thing.

❖ Offer to care for any other pets.

❖ Offer to drive your friend to the veterinarian.

❖ Give your friend a copy of this book.

❖ Send a sympathy card or flowers.

❖ Locate a pet loss support group, and accompany your friend to the meeting.

❖ Don't suggest that your friend immediately get a new pet.

❖ Don't surprise your friend with a new pet.

❖ Do expect your friend to feel sad for quite a few months. (The grief should diminish in intensity over time).

❖ Validate your friend's right to grieve for as long as needed.

Personal Growth From Grief and Loss. Sometimes, after the intense grieving has subsided, pet owners realize that the loss experience has changed them for the better.

For example, Mary, a professional singer, noted that a year after her llama, Roberto, died, her singing had a much better tone and quality than ever before in her career. She attributed this improvement to the fact that she had gained a greater understanding of herself, of life, and of death, as she shared Roberto's euthanasia experience, healed from her grief, and faced the continued adventure of life's challenges. Mary liked to say that her career advancement was her personal memorial to the memory of Roberto.

TO THINK ABOUT.   What are your plans for how you will use the time and energy you used to share with your pet? How will you keep your pet's memory alive? How will you find support for yourself? When will you start to put your plans into effect?

CHAPTER 20

A MEDITATION FOR THE END
OF YOUR PET'S LIFE

(Dots indicate spots where the reader should pause for 20 seconds)

Start by sitting quietly and taking a few deep breaths . . . Let yourself feel comfortable and relaxed. . . .

And now imagine, in your mind's eye, that you are walking down a shady, tree-lined path that leads to a large building off in the distance. . . . As you approach the building, you realize it is a library . . . a very special kind of library. The books in this library contain the life of every pet who has ever been given the mission of living a lifetime with a human. In this library, you will find a book with your pet's name embossed in gold on the front cover.

You enter the library, and search through the shelves of books until you find your pet's lifebook . . . you open the cover, and on the first page you see pictures of your pet from the first instant he came into your life . . . Just the way he looked the first time you saw him . . . How he responded to you, . . . And how you felt . . . Do you remember?

What was that like when you were getting to know each other? . . . And finding activities you could share . . . What things did you have fun doing together? . . . Take some time to remember. . . .

You turn the pages, and there your pet is a little older, and still so beautiful. . . . In your mind's eye, picture just how your pet looked when he was at his best. . . .

Remember how your pet communicated with you. . . . What sounds did your pet made when he was happy? . . . When he was sad? . . .

What did you especially like about your pet's unique personality? What special or funny things did he do? . . .

Remember what you did to care for your pet. . . . What were his favorite foods? . . . his special toys? . . . any special clothing? . . . See if there are pictures of you caring for your pet in his lifebook. . . .

How did your pet care for you? . . . What did he teach you? . . . Are there pictures of your pet caring for you . . . Comforting you . . . listening to you . . . kissing you . . . being there for you when no one else was . . . Take time and remember. . . .

The pictures in your pet's lifebook continue on through all the years you and your pet have had together, . . . Everything you did – the funny times, . . . The hard times . . . All the things you shared, . . . until now . . . the ending of your pet's life.

Allow yourself to feel the happiness and magic you two have shared, . . . and allow yourself to feel the sadness . . . now, as your pet's life draws to its close. . . .

You turn the page, and there are no more pictures, just some writing. Your animal friend has written some thoughts he wants to share with you as his life is ending:

Dear Human Friend,

"I want you to understand that I have lived my life, and it is now drawing to its close. My life span is shorter than a human's. I am sad about that reality. But I accept it, and want you to accept it. I hope you can let go and give me permission to die as I approach the end of my life. Whether you choose euthanasia to end my suffering, or let death come at it's own time, I want you to know that an animal does not fear death as some humans do. Death is a natural event which I accept.

I have held on to my life as long as possible because of my worry about how you will get along without me. But, because you have learned to care so well for me, I have faith that you will find a way to care for yourself when my physical presence is no longer there to comfort you. I know that my spirit and the memory of our few brief years together will remain with you to strengthen you in the hard times that are ahead when the two of us must part.

I want you to share this final experience with me to the extent that you can let yourself. I don't ask for a longer life, or a medical miracle. I know when you do the medical tests and treatments, you do them to keep me with you. So I put up with them – to stay with you longer. But I could do without all the medical fuss. All I really want, as I am dying, is for you to be with me and lovingly comfort me. That is one of the last pictures I want in this lifebook – the two of us sharing this final experience as I prepare to go to the land of the spirit at Rainbow Bridge where I will wait for you.

I want you to find companionship to fill the time we two have always spent together. We both know another pet will never measure up to me. But I understand your need for an animal companion. So, in time, I will send another animal friend who needs your love and care, and a new lifebook will be started. . . . But not just yet. For now, seek out human friends. Connect with the best in these humans as you share your grief with those who understand what it is like for one left behind after the death of a pet.

I have left the final page of this lifebook empty for a picture of you, my beloved owner. I will have accomplished my mission if that final picture shows you taking care of yourself as well as you have always cared for me. Remember me and celebrate my life, and our lives together. But do not cling to the past. Embrace life. Explore new directions to focus your life, and search out new loving relationships after I leave you. In doing so, you will best honor my memory. And I will be at peace."

APPENDIX

Resources for Pet Bereavement Counseling:

The **Animal Medical Center**, New York, New York.
Phone: (212) 838-8100.
Colorado State University, School of Veterinary Medicine.
Fort Collins, CO. Phone: (303) 221-4535.
University of California, School of Veterinary Medicine.
Davis, CA. (916) 752-4200.
University of Pennsylvania, School of Veterinary Medicine,
Philadelphia, PA. Phone: (215) 898-4525.
Washington State University.
Pullman, WA. Phone: (509) 335-1297.

Here you will find pet loss support groups, and short-term pet loss counseling, usually with no charge or a small charge.

A Pet Loss Crisis Line is available at the University of California School of Veterinary Medicine in Davis, California.
(916) 752-4200. In operation M-F 5:30-9:30 PM Pacific Standard Time. No Charge.

PetFriends, Inc. Compassionate telephone support for pet owners in grief. New Jersey regional pet loss support. Phone: 1-800-404-pets.

The Delta Society, 289 Perimeter Road East, Renton, WA. 98055-1329, Phone: (206) 226-7357, Fax: (206) 235-1076, E-Mail: Deltasociety @cis.compuserve.com   is a non-profit organization concerned about people, animals, and the environment. They sell an **educational packet** entitled *Pet Loss and Bereavement,* and publish an annual **directory of resources and professional counselors** throughout the United States who do pet loss counseling or have pet loss support groups available. Expect to pay for much of the counseling listed in this directory.

The International Association of Pet Cemeteries,
Phone: 1-800-952-5541.

BIBLIOGRAPHY

Further Suggested Reading:

How to Survive the Loss of a Love, Melba Colgrove, et al.
   New York: Prelude Press, 1991. 212 pages.

Living When a Loved One Has Died. Earl Grollman.
   Boston: Beacon Press, 1977. 113 pages.

When Bad Things Happen to Good People. H.S.Kushner.
   New York: Schocken, 1981.

The Souls of Animals. Gary Kowalski.
   Walpole, N.H.: Stillpoint, 1991. 114 pages

A Final Act of Caring. Mary and Herb Montgomery.
   Minneapolis: Montgomery Press, 1993. 32 pages.

When Your Pet Dies: How to Cope With Your Feelings.
   Jamie Quackenbush. New York: Pocket Books, 1985. 223 pages.

By Penelope Smith: *Animal Death: A Spiritual Journey*. (Audiotape).
Animals...Our Return to Wholeness. (Book). *Species Link* (Quarterly
Journal).
   Pegasus Publications, Point Reyes, CA. Phone: 1-800-356-9315.

For Children:

A Special Place For Charlie. Debby Morehead.
   Broomfield, Co.: Partners in Publishing, 1996, 28 pages (dog).

Sunflower Mountain. Kathleen Foster-Morgan.
   Toronto: Sunflower Publications, 1995, 32 pages.

The Tenth Best Thing About Barney. Judith Viorst.
   New York: Macmillan, 1971, 24 pages (cat).

Old Yeller. Fred Gipson.
   New York: Harper, 1956, 158 pages (dog).

INDEX